# Bertha's Book

## A View of Starksboro's History

## By Bertha B. Hanson – 1917-1994

### Compiled by Emma-Lou G. Craig

Starksboro Village Meeting House Society - Starksboro, Vermont 05487

**Bertha's Book**
160 pages
ISBN 0-9663025-0-8
Printing:  Thomson-Shore, Inc.

Book/Cover Design:  Linda Williamson
                    Dawson Design

The Vermont Division for Historic Preservation
has granted permission to reprint pages
237 to 242 of:
Vermont Division for Historic Preservation
*The Historic Architecture of Addison County*
Montpelier, Vt. 1992.
This excerpt is found at the end of this book.

# Table of Contents

# Introduction

For years, most people in Starksboro, Huntington, and Monkton were able to "Ask Bertha" whenever they had a question about how old their house was, where someone lived...when Starksboro was settled, information about any of the 17 schools in Starksboro or the 4-5 churches and on and on....if Bertha didn't know, which usually was unlikely, she'd have the information for you within a few days. At various gatherings she would provide several large albums of wonderful old photographs with captions on them about their age, location and particular interesting details about their construction. She always was there to keep our history available to us and made it such interesting reading.

Naturally everyone wanted Bertha to write a history as she knew so much about our town. She was always very busy with her many commitments and meetings. One only has to read Elsa Gilbertson's tribute to her in the 1993 Town Report to glean why she probably never got around to writing the History.

Fortunately, we have people like Elsa Gilbertson who is a valuable resource for similar information, Bertha's children who listened to her stories over and over again, and her mother-in-law, Olive Hanson, who recalls much of Starksboro's history. We also are fortunate to have several senior citizens who recall much of Starksboro's past.

This is not Starksboro's history as Bertha would have written it, but it is Bertha's writings in the Town Reports as they were written from 1954 -1994. They are listed in this publication in the order as written by Bertha, thus the headings for each "Chapter". Gathering the photos that were in her collected albums, appropriate pictures have been combined with *the subjects she was writing about for each year's Town Report. Each historic photo of a building has a number in parentheses which corresponds to the State Register of Historic Places listings and maps in the back of the book provided by the Vermont Division for Historic Preservation.*

*Bertha's Book would not have been possible without the skills and talents of Linda Williamson who has been the creative designer who has scanned all the photographs, made suggestions and tended to all the tedious details of layout and organization that make the book so readable.*

*Elsa Gilbertson and Olive Phillips (one of Bertha's daughters) have been wonderful at responding to calls in hours of panic over a caption, a circa date, or location of particular photographs as well as constant en-couragement and suggestions. Thank you Elsa, Linda, and Olive, personal friends and family, and everyone in town who have added encouraging support for this project as well as special thanks to Katie and Doug Campbell for their diligent proof-reading and support.*

*We hope you enjoy perusing Bertha's legacy.*

*Emma-Lou Gale Craig*

✱ Numbers in photograph captions refer to the maps and lists on pages 146 to 153 reprinted with permission from the Vermont Division for Historic Preservation, *The Historic Architecture of Addison County.*

Starksboro, as originally chartered, was first settled by George Bidwell and Horace Kellogg. George Bidwell located on the farm where Nobel Wyman's tenement house is now situated, while Horace Kellogg settled where Kenneth Besaw now lives.

They left Connecticut in August, 1787 and upon arriving in Starksboro camped east of the present location of the Wyman tenement house. After clearing two acres of land and laying up the body of a log hut they returned to Connecticut.

In March of the following year, George Bidwell, accompanied by his wife and two children, again set out for Starksboro. On April 7, 1788 they reached their new home which was then several miles from the nearest neighbor. At the spot where the house now stands they set up the sled boards and some bark thus providing shelter for the first two weeks. The following spring a small house was built. The frame is part of the house now standing on the place. About 1795 the family opened their home as a tavern and continued to entertain travelers there until about 1820.

Horace Kellogg and his family arrived in town at about the same time, perhaps accompanying the Bidwells on the journey from Connecticut. Hannah Kellogg was thought by some to have been the first child born in town but the first date that can be established is that for Cyrus Bidwell, December 11, 1790. The first marriage was that of David Kellogg and Christiana Traver, March 3, 1793.

Submitted by
Bertha Hanson
Town Report 1954

In 1797 a large tract of land lying east of Hogsback Mountain was annexed to Starksboro. Roughly included within this area was the part of the town now located west of a line beginning a short distance northeast of Floyd Shepard's house, passing through Starksboro village near Harry Strong's store, and continuing to the Bristol line.

This section was first settled by John Ferguson who came from Nine Partners', New York. He located in the vicinity of Starksboro village. Though the date of his settlement is unknown, he was chosen as one of Monkton's first selectmen on March 28, 1786. At about the same time Thomas Vradenburg settled near the Bristol line. In 1792 Samuel Hall built the house now occupied by Leslie Hollis.

John Ferguson became impressed by the inconvenience it caused the people east of Hogsback Mountain to reach the business center of Monkton. While representing that town in the legislature he successfully used his influence in getting that area annexed to Starksboro. In 1798 he became Starksboro's first representative. On the brook above Ernest Eddy's he operated the first Grist Mill and Fulling Mill in town.

As early as 1815 Samuel Bushnell operated a blacksmith shop west of the present site of Harry Strong's store. About 1819, in partnership with Elisha Ferguson, he built a forge on the farm now occupied by Leroy Smith. They also operated a furnace about half a mile east of the village. Later the furnace was moved to a location west of Harry Strong's present store. At an early date, Elisha Ferguson kept a store and operated a wheelwright shop where Harold Clifford now lives.

In 1831 George Ferguson began the manufacture of carriages and in 1868 a carriage shop, which is now Amos Hanson's barn, was built. For many years O.D. Baldwin operated a sawmill and buttertub factory as well as a cheese factory on the stream above the village. He also developed the trout pond known as "Baldwin's Pond."

Submitted by
Bertha Hanson
Town Report 1955

**John Ferguson  1753-1815**
*First settler in Starksboro Village.*
*Settled in the part of Monkton next to*
*Starksboro in 1797.*
*Selectman in Monkton in 1787.*
*He developed the water power in what is now*
*Starksboro Village.*
*Established a saw mill on what is now*
*Tatro Road in Starksboro.*
*First Representative in 1798.*

**Amy (Cuthbert) Haight Ferguson  1757-1839**
*Second wife of John Ferguson.*
*Clerk for the Proprietors of Monkton.*

*Grist Mill Operator's House, c.1810/c.1900. This was originally a Cape Cod style house built in the very early 1800s for the operator of the Grist Mill across the stream. It was wonderfully remodeled c.1900 in the Queen Anne style by Madge & Ernest Eddy and her father, Cornelius Ladoo. They added the bands of shingles, windows with stained glass, and the porch with its turned columns and shingled apron. Ladoo was responsible for building the stone walls lining the banks of Baldwin's Brook which by the late 1800s had become a number of muddy rivulets. Just to the East of the house was the site of a tannery run in the mid-1800s by James Washurne. (Now home of Norma Wedge.)* **(A13)**

*Wentworth Hotel, c.1835* This grand old house, located at the heart of the village, was once Wentworth's Hotel and was in operation until the 1860s when it became a private home. The land, bought by Asahel Wentworth in 1811, was called "the Tavern Stand" in 1835 when his estate was settled. This reference may be to this building or an earlier one on the site. The old hotel still retains its Greek Revival style doorway framed by sidelights and pilasters, the "double-decker" pilasters on the corner, and the peaked lintel boards over the windows. *(Now owned by John Parker.)* **(A8)**

*Village Scene looking North – Starksboro, Vt.*

**Ferguson Grist Mill/Carriage Shop, c.1795/1868.** *This well-preserved building on its high stone foundation was one of the first grist mills in town, and is another exceptional structure that vividly tells part of the town's history. It was begun by John Ferguson possibly before 1800. Upstream from this he built a sawmill and an iron forge. His grandson, George W., started making carriages in 1831 in the old grist mill. Between 1838 and 1854 David worked with his cousin Charles. They also made coffins. (Now owned by Jonathan & Marlene Tierney.)* **(A14)**

**Baptist Church 1869.** **(A20)**

***L. Taft Store/Cyrus W. Atwood House, c.1830/later additions.*** *Originally this was a one story building, with an attached wheelwright shop run by George Ferguson. It was converted to a dwelling by 1857, and was bought in 1849 by Lee Taft, who ran a store and the post office here. The 1871 map shows this as the home of Cyrus W. Atwood, who kept the store next door. (Now home of Daniel Harris & Kristen Hendee.)* **(A33)**

**(A33)**

***Sidney Sayles House/ Walston's Hotel, c.1840/ c.1890.*** *This spacious house, possibly built c.1840 for Sidney Sayles, has a typical Greek Revival style doorway framed by sidelights and entry pilasters. Like several other village buildings, it was transformed in the late 1800s (when it was Walston's Hotel) by the addition of a second story. (Now home of Reginald & Mary Wedge.)*

**(A35)**

**(A35)**

**Watering Trough** *at the foot of Big Hollow Rd. across from the Starksboro Village Store.*

*Dr. Abel Sweet/Dr. William Gregory House, c.1800.* *This is one of the oldest houses in the village. It is a simple Cape Cod type and was probably built c.1800 by John Ferguson. Ferguson sold it at an early date. It has been the home to two doctors in its history – Dr. Abel Sweet, who lived here by 1848, and Dr. William Gregory, noted here on an 1871 map. (Now the home of Mark Lathrop.)* **(A30)**

The first settlement in South Starksboro was made by Philander Orvis sometime between 1795 and 1800. He purchased one-hundred acres of land on the farm now occupied by Sarah Orvis, built a house and started making improvements, only to find that his title to the property was invalid. Subsequently he had to repurchase his farm. At an early date he and his brother Loren built the first saw mill in that part of town on the nearby stream.

In 1800 Robert Young from Sheldon, Vermont settled on the farm which Herman Orvis now owns. The country was then so wild that on one occasion his wife, Hannah, was obliged to defend their stock from an attack by wolves armed only with a pitchfork.

With the arrival of more settlers small industries were established on the streams. The brothers, Thomas, David and Ephraim Morrison, came from New Hampshire in 1808. They started a tannery on the stream just above the Bristol line. Later they began the manufacture of rakes, doing all the work by hand. In the early days they carried their goods to market in Vergennes and New Haven on horseback. The business changed hands several times and was a thriving enterprise for many years. Under the management of J.H. Orvis, fork and hoe handles were also manufactured.

By 1870 there were several successful industries in the region. S.R. Cain operated a stave mill which employed ten men and made about 12,000 staves a day. Buell and Morrison, later Buell, Thompson & Co., manufactured about 10,000 butter tubs annually. Daniel Orvis operated a saw mill and just below it a grist mill.

For many years a post office was located near S.R. Cain's stave mill. Later it was moved to J.W. Orvis' store. He was postmaster for many years.

Many of the early residents were Quakers. During the early years they were associated with the church in Lincoln. In 1871, however, the Friends' church in South Starksboro, built in 1825, was remodeled at a cost of approximately $1,000.00.

Submitted by,
Bertha B. Hanson
1956 Town Report

***West School.*** *(Now the home of Sarah & Mark Adams.)* **(52)**

***Robert Young House.*** *Situated on site of present house this one burned about 1930. (Now the home of Larry & Susan Shephard.)* **(32)**

***Grace Hallock's Home, c.1865.*** *Ira Hallock with the horses. This has been the home of several generations of the family. (Now the home of Alissa Close & Christopher Brady.)* **(25)**

*Sawmill in South Starksboro.* Possibly Bunker Mill in So. Starksboro which would have been located actoss from what is now Stark Mt. Tennis Assn. Probably Noah Lafayette is driving the team.

*Lincoln Friends Meeting House.* Attended by South Starksboro Quakers.

***Herman Orvis Place.*** *About 1920. Originally the "Old Robert Young Home", this was the place settled by the first Robert Young when he came to Starksboro. One of the oldest houses in South Starksboro. (Now the home of Dorothy Orvis.)*

***Zita Heffernan House,*** *c.1860. Located on Lafayette Road in South Starksboro.* **(33)**

***The Joe Lafayette Place.*** *Once located on Lafayette Road in South Starksboro. No longer there.*

***Earl Siples House*** *on Dan Sargent Rd.  Present home of Dan & Alice Dubenetsky*

The section of Starksboro known as "Hillsboro" originally included roughly the area between the Hannon farm now owned by the town and the corner above the Ireland school house. The first deed to property in this area was given to Samuel Hill of Barrington, New Hampshire, on June 22, 1798. This was to land near the former Hillsboro school house. The following year his cousin, John, purchased land near the twin bridges.

The exact date when the brothers moved their families to Vermont is not clear. However, by the time the U.S. census for 1800 was taken, Samuel, his wife, and their six children, her cousin John and his wife, and also two other brothers, William and Thomas, who later purchased land near-by, were living in Starksboro. That year another brother, Lemuel, settled on the farm now known as the Morton Hill place. The last of the family to locate in town was Francis, who, in 1810, purchased land above the present location of the Ireland school house.

According to tradition, Samuel moved his goods through the woods from New Hampshire on a hand sled. At the time he began clearing his land the nearest neighbor was three miles away. In 1805 he became the second man to represent Starksboro in the state legislature.

Hillsboro was isolated by its location from activities in other parts of town. As early as 1817, Rev. Bowles, an itinerant Baptist minister, began holding church services in the homes of families in that neighborhood. In September, 1821, the Baptist church was organized with 17 members. No church building was erected, however, until the present one was built at the village in 1869.

Changing social and economic conditions led many of the second generation to move away from the hill farms. Some went west, some went to other towns, others bought land in the valley. By 1870 there was only one Hill family living in Hillsboro. Many of our townspeople, however, number one or more of the Hill brothers among their ancestors.

As submitted by
Bertha B. Hanson
1957 Town Report

*Haying in Hillsboro.*

**Joseph & Catherine Hill Home, Hillsboro.** *Now the Fish & Game parking lot.*

*Lemuel Hill Farm, c.1810.*
*Ell since torn off. New*
*home of Elise Olson.* **(35)**

***Barns on Old Nathan***
***Morrison Farm.***
*David Dike with oxen.*
*Farm is now owned by*
*Vermont Forest &*
*Parks and the*
*buildings are gone.*

Rockville and States Prison Hollow owe their early settlement and rapid development to the abundant water power available at the Great Falls of Lewis Creek. As early as 1793 David Hoag, Elihu Hoag and Stephen Carpenter formed a company and purchased the land now roughly comprising this area.

They immediately set about establishing industries along the stream. By 1799 the grist mill, now Mr. Adsit's Old Mill Workshop, was completed. Above this a saw mill had already been constructed. Next, with the assistance of Giles Hard, a fulling and carding mill was erected on the north side of the stream just below the grist mill. This was leased to Giles Hard in 1805. By 1812 Jonathan Alger and Jonathan Varney had completed a forge further down the stream. This, too, was operated by agreement with David Hoag & Company.

In later years, Paine & Harkness operated a foundry and plow manufacturing company in States Prison Hollow. This was located on the east bank of Beaver Brook near its junction with Lewis Creek.

These thriving industries attracted settlers to this section of town. In 1802 Daniel Peake purchased land on the west bank of Lewis Creek on the States Prison Hollow Road. Benjamin Taber settled nearby in 1809. David Meader bought land near the present location of Green Mountain Creamery. Joshua Varney lived on the former Frank Wells farm, Joel Battey where Carroll Zeno now lives, William Hanson on the farm now owned by Joseph Hendee. Almond Atwood and George Harkness located on the farm now occupied by Clifford Hanson.

*Steven Jennings Place.*

17

**Clinton Jennings Place.** *Probably built by George Harkness, this house is located in States Prison Hollow. At the time the picture was taken, the Jody Morrill family lived there.*

These families, as well as several others living nearby, were members of the Society of Friends. On April 6, 1804 a committee representing the Monkton Monthly Meeting of Friends purchased the "Meeting House Lot", now a part of Green Mountain Cemetery. In 1812 a church was built there and the Monthly Meeting of the Society of Friends in Starksboro was organized.

With changing economic conditions small industries began to decline. Then, too, several Quaker families moved to western New York. By 1858 the membership in the Quaker church was so small that the building was sold and removed to Charlotte where it is now part of the Catholic Church. One by one the shops along the creek were abandoned. Only the old grist mill now remains.

As submitted by
Bertha B. Hanson
1958 Town Report

**States Prison Hollow after the Flood of 1938.**

**Home of Grace & Oliver Besaw.** *Located north of Varney Hill below Zeno's Farm.*

**Mark Hill Place.** *Now the home of Ralph & Martha Cota. This farm was settled by members of the Battey Family. Charles M. H. Ferguson lived there for many years. Later it was owned by Hervey & Lois Hill, then by their son Mark, and his wife Belle. Ernest Pecor owned it for several years and it then became the property of Arthur & Vera Cota.*

**Atwood Place.** *Now the home of Norman & Diane Cota.*

**Residence of Ruthena Zeno.** *Built by Nicholas Battey, it was later owned by three generations of Hill's – Harry M., Henry M. and Dayton J. Hill. Picture taken about 1926 when Lester Keys owned the place.*

*Prison Hollow Road* on left. Home of Norman and Diane Cota on right.

*William Worth House, c.1840.* Richard Worth, an early village settler who drafted the first plan of the town on calf skin, owned much of the southern end of the village. His son William lived in this house, a fine example of the Greek Revival style. William held many town offices and in 1868 wrote a history of the town for Abby Hemenway's Gazetteer. This property is also significant for its collection of old barns and outbuildings. Now the home of David & Bette Mason. **(A21)**

There are the Redcoats and they are ours, or this night Molly Stark sleeps a widow!" With these words General John Stark led his small, inadequately equipped force of farmers to victory against the British regulars in the Battle of Bennington on August 16, 1777.

At this time it was becoming apparent that settlers would soon be moving into the wilderness of northern Vermont. Prominent men, desirous of making money, formed companies and petitioned the legislature for grants of townships in the new area. In 1778 a company led by Brig. Gen. John Stark petitioned for a tract of land near Hancock which they requested be named Stark's Town. At about the same time two petitions, one from David Bridia and Daniel Smith, the other from Joseph Bowker and Associates, were received each requesting a grant to an area roughly comparable to that now comprising Starksboro.

Though there is no record that any action was taken concerning these petitions, on Nov. 7, 1780 the Town of Starksboro was granted to sixty-six men, among them David Bridia, Brig. Gen. John Stark, Joseph Bowker

and Daniel Smith. Two days later a charter was issued to the new town. Thus Starksboro, which lies in the shadow of the "three Starks", the Green Mountain Peaks known as John Stark, Baby Stark, and Molly Stark, came into being.

Names for new towns were chosen by Gov. Chittenden and his council under legislative authority. Often towns were named for prominent individuals or for one of the proprietors. Obviously, in the case of Starksboro, this double honor fell to Brig. Gen. John Stark.

In the divisions of land John Stark received 1st Div. Lot No 68, part of which, at least, is included in the farm now owned by Arthur Cota, 2nd Div. Lot 25, in the Shaker Hill region, and 3rd Div. Lot No. 24, located in the area between Hillsborough and Brown Hill.

Proprietors seldom visited their lands. As soon as possible they sold their property to settlers. However, it is interesting to note that there is a tradition that John Stark once camped south of Starksboro Village near the farms now owned by Earl Kelley and Keith Besaw.

As submitted by
Bertha Hanson
1959 Town Report

Elder Charles Bowles, an itinerant minister of the Free Will Baptist faith, began holding services in Starksboro in 1817. Meetings were held at the Hillsboro School House, the Brown Hill School House or in the homes of interested persons whenever Elder Bowles was in that locality.

On September 21, 1821, at a meeting held on Brown Hill, seventeen people joined hands "in token of their union and fellowship". Elder Bowles gave them the hand of fellowship and declared them a church of the Free Will Baptist order.

For many years Monthly Meetings were held alternately in the school houses at Hillsboro and Brown Hill. By 1865, however, the majority of the members had moved into the valley. More and more frequently their meetings were held at the South Village School House, located near the Hillsboro turn in what is now Keith Besaw's lower meadow, or at the North Red School House. Although the Baptists were privileged to use the Village Meeting House, now known as the Community House, a part of the time it was apparent that they needed a building of their own.

The first meeting of the Free Will Baptist Meeting House Association was held on February 4, 1868. Deacon John True Hill was appointed a trustee to take deeds of land from Martin Mead and William Worth "in trust for the first Freewill Baptist Church in Starksboro." Benjamin Knight, William Worth and Sylvannus Hill were chosen to draft a subscription for raising funds with which to construct a new building. The sum of $6,648.00 was raised by receiving bids on the fifty pews or "slips" in the audience room. The prices paid for each pew ranged from $50.00 to $350.00. The bell was selected by Benjamin Knight. Erwin Lamos, a former Starksboro resident well known as a scene painter for the Boston Museum, was engaged to "grain" the wood work in the audience room.

By the fall of 1869 the Meeting House grounds were fenced and graded. On December 15 of that year "a large and interesting" audience listened to the dedication sermon preached by Rev. Marrinor, a minister from Massachusetts.

Few changes were made in the building during the first forty-five years. By 1915, however, it was felt that the church should be brought up to date. During 1915 and 1916 several changes were made. Stained glass replaced the old clear windows, a new choir loft was built, the audience room was repainted and the baptistry was installed in the lower room.

On January 29, 1917 the newly redeco-
rated church was officially incorporated under Vermont law. The name was changed
to The First Baptist Church of Starksboro.

As submitted by
Bertha B. Hanson
1960 Town Report

**Baptist Church Horse Sheds.**
*Pictured is Phyllis Tobin, Norma
Wedge's sister.*

***First Free Will Baptist Church,
1868.** The Free Will Baptists were
organized in 1821 by Rev. Sylvanus
Robertson and Rev. Charles Bowles,
who was the son of a white woman
and a black slave. The Baptists met
in barns, groves, and schoolhouses,
before they joined the Methodist
Episcopals and the Christian
congregations in building the
Meeting House in 1838. The Free
Will Baptist Meeting House
Association built this church in
1869 at a cost of nearly $7,000.
It is Greek Revival in style.* **(A20)**

Rev. Joseph Mitchell organized the Methodist Episcopal Church in Starksboro in 1798. The first meetings were held at the home of Abraham Bushnell who settled at the top of the Village Hill on the farm later known as the "Holcomb Place". Often no minister was present at the meetings. Mrs. Bushnell persuaded Elijah Hedding, a wild young man who was an excellent reader, to read sermons to those gathered in her home. He became converted and was baptized in the nearby brook. The stone upon which he knelt during the ceremony was subsequently engraved with the date. For many years it was to be seen in a nearby wall. Rev. Elijah Hedding became a prominent Bishop in the Methodist Episcopal Church. He served in the Troy Conference until his death in 1852.

Membership in the Methodist Church, the Baptist Church and the Christian Church increased rapidly. The need for a meeting house became apparent. An organization known as The Village Meeting House Society was formed. In 1838 this society secured from Myron Holcomb and Ira Bushnell deeds to adjoining tracts of land in Starksboro Village. On this property a meeting house was erected. The building, completed in 1840, at a cost of $2,400.00, had seating room for 240 persons. It is said that Sidney Bushnell and Oscar Baldwin were chosen to go to Troy, N.Y. to purchase the fine toned bell. Before the days of telephones and daily papers the bell was tolled at nine o'clock on the morning following a death in the community. The number of times it was struck made known the age and sex of the deceased.

The basement of the Village Meeting House provided a gathering place for the townspeople. Until the present town hall was built town meetings were held there. The long benches in the lower rooms were built by George Ferguson, whose brother, Rev. David Ferguson, was for many years minister of the church.

In the early years the Methodists had the use of the church one-half the time, the Baptists one-fourth the time and the Christian Church one-fourth the time. The Baptists later built their own meeting house and the Christian Church became inactive. The Methodist Church was left in sole possession of the building.

During the early years of the present century, stained glass windows, given as memorials to those who helped to found and maintain the Methodist Episcopal

Church in Starksboro, replaced the shuttered windows. The church kitchen and parlors were remodeled and furnace installed.

In 1919 the Methodists ceased to hold meetings. The Village Meeting House, no longer used for church purposes, became the property of the newly organized Starksboro Community Club in 1957. The Village Meeting House is now known once again as the Starksboro Village Meeting House.

As submitted by
Bertha B. Hanson

1961 Town Report

*Starksboro Village Meeting House, 1838-1840. This church, listed in the National Register of Historic Places, is an excellent example of Gothic Revival style architecture. It was built between 1838 and 1840 by the Methodist Episcopal, Free Will Baptist, and Christian congregations, and by the Town, which appropriated $400 to furnish the basement room for use as the Town Hall. The stained glass window panes were added in 1916-17 when the audience room was remodeled.* **(A29)**

***David Ferguson House, c. 1810/c. 1965.***
*David Ferguson was deeded this property for $100 in 1831 by his father Elisha Ferguson, who got it from his father John. David, who had many talents, was an ordained Methodist minister and made plows for many years. This house was completed remodeled by Joe Pechie, who bought it in 1962. Now the home of Mary O'Brien and Mark Lucas.* **(A16)**

***George W. Ferguson House, c. 1810.*** *This probably is two houses that were joined together in the 19th century. It was originally owned by John Ferguson. His grandson, George W. Ferguson, who made carriages and coffins next door is shown living here in 1857 and 1871 maps of the village. The stone wall in front of this house and the next was built by Hervey Hanson for the State in the mid-1930s when the road was paved. Now the home of Jonathan and Marlaine Tierney. (Ruth Baldwin is standing next to the tree.)* **(A15)**

27

*Both photos are of the Abraham Bushnell Place at the foot of Brown Hill.* Now owned by John and Laura Lomas. Barns no longer exist. **(16)**

28

***Abraham Bushnell Place*** *at the foot of Brown Hill.* **(16)**

***Hill and Miles Sawmill.*** *Located where the Adsit Camp now stands. Lyman Hill and Mr. Miles operated a successful sawmill there for many years. Now the site of John & Gretchen Adsit's home.*

Starksboro was chartered by the State of Vermont, November 9, 1780. Twice since that time the area of the town has been increased by territory annexed from Monkton.

On March 4, 1797, by act of the Vermont Legislature, 2,726 acres of land were taken from the east side of Monkton and added to Starksboro. Prior to that time, the Starksboro-Monkton line had begun at a point roughly somewhat east of Kenneth Gardner's house. Extending northward, it crossed Harold Shivarette's pasture where the old line markers may still be seen, and passed through Starksboro Village a short distance east of Frank Strong's store. This line was moved to the west about 320 rods so that it now extends along the east slope of Hogback Mountain.

The first settler in this area was John Ferguson, proprietors' clerk of Monkton and also a surveyor. He recorded the first survey of his Monkton property in 1787. Within a few years he had acquired extensive holdings in what is now Starksboro Village. His home farm was that now owned by Leroy Smith. (Hank & Cecilia Bissell)

Soon afterward Thomas Vradenburg, another early settler in this area, located near the Bristol line. James Hedding, father of Bishop Hedding, is said to have settled on the farm now occupied by Harland Saunders. Austin Bostwick and Joseph Worth also settled in this section. The oldest house in town, that now occupied by Earl Brown, is said to have been built by Samuel Hall in 1797.

Daniel Peake of Ferrisburg acquired land on the slope west of States Prison Hollow north of the present highway in 1790. His descendants lived for many years beside the "Peake Hill" road which is now a part of Clifford Hanson's pasture.

Settlers on the east side of Hogback Mountain found it inconvenient to attend meetings in Monkton because of the distance they had to travel. John Ferguson, as representative from Monkton, was instrumental in introducing in the Vermont Legislature the bill to have the land east of the mountain annexed to Starksboro.

About 1909 the Vermont Legislature again added a strip of Monkton land to Starksboro. This piece, 160 rods deep, extended northerly from the stone wall north of Floyd Shepard's house to the Hinesburg line.

Among the early settlers in this section was Andrew Frank of Caanan, Connecticut. In 1794, he purchased land which included the property where Chase Stokes now lives. James Lamos from Barnstead, New Hampshire, bought the place where Roy Carlson lives in 1807. At an early date, James Ross of Leicester, Vermont, purchased land which is now a part of Nobel Wyman's farm. Joseph and Nathan Rounds lived on the west side of Lewis Creek, beside the "Monkton Cross road". There, in Nobel Wyman's pasture is a small burial plot where members of the Rounds family are buried.

As submitted by
Bertha B. Hanson
1962 Town Report

*Conway Place, 1797/c.1926.* Built in 1797, remodeled in 1926, this was the first frame house in Starksboro located at the corner of Tatro Road and Route 116. Now an apartment house owned by Muriel Brown. **(53)**

**John Ferguson House, c. 1810.** *The rear section is the oldest part of the house and was lived in by the first settler in the village, John Ferguson. He was the town's first representative, started one of the first grist mills, and also had a forge and trip hammer shop, and a fulling mill. A large part of the village was originally Ferguson's farm. Elisha and Samuel Bushnell began an iron foundry on the farm in 1819. Hoel Sayles "kept transient guests" here in the early 1870s when there was no operating hotel in the village. He also built the large barn which is still being used. Now Lewis Creek Farm and the home of Hank and Cecilia Bissell.* **(A38)**

*Leroy Smith and Edgar Smith with oxen.*

***Noble Wyman Place, c.1840.*** *Located on Wyman Hill on Route 116. Ell was removed in the 1940s. Located in the part of Monkton set to Starksboro in 1909. Now owned by Will and Kathleen Ramsay.* **(7)**

*Noble Wyman Place - Wyman Hill - Route 116, c.1840.* Now the home of William & Kathleen Ramsey. **(7)**

*William Wyman Place - Wyman Hill - Route 116, c.1880/c.1900.* Home of Evelyn Nelson & Mitch Kelly. **(8)**

The section of Starksboro known as Little Ireland was settled by immigrants who left their homeland in the mid-nineteenth century. During the years 1845-47 a severe blight destroyed the potato crop, the main staple of diet in Ireland. The terrible famine which ensued, together with an acute shortage of agricultural land, resulted in a huge exodus to America.

First to arrive in Starksboro was Thomas Hannon from County Limerick. He reached America in 1847 and is said to have come to Starksboro in 1848. He was soon followed by Francis and Ellen Hannon. Their son, Thomas who was born in 1852, was the first Catholic child born in town. At about the same time Thomas Casey, a stone mason from County Claire settled here. Among other early arrivals were the families of James Conway from County Limerick, Timothy Butler, John O'Connor, John Welch, John Murphy, Thomas Dillon, John Fitzgerald, Patrick Coughlin, Daniel Hayes, Andrew Halpin and Patrick Leonard.

Much of the land purchased by these families was unimproved. Trees had to be cut, homes built and land brought under cultivation. It is said that a saw mill was set up at an early date to prepare lumber for building purposes.

The growing population soon made it necessary to establish School District No. 11. A school house was built on the corner where the Conway turn joins the highway leading to Hillsboro. For many years this building also served as a church.

In 1854 Rev. Thomas Reiordan celebrated the first Mass in town. After that time stations were given from Burlington and Middlebury. Even so the services of the Church often seemed far removed from the little community. In order to have her eldest child, Thomas, baptized as soon as possible, Ellen Stapleton Hannon, wife of Thomas (first Catholic child born in town) walked the twenty-three miles to Burlington carrying the infant in her arms. The first Catholic baptism in Starksboro was that of Annora Casey, daughter of Michael and Alice Casey. The first Catholic marriage was that of John Maher and Bridget Golden with the Rev. Michael McAuley officiating.

Little Ireland became a thriving agricultural community. For many years Thomas Casey operated a creamery which was located near the school house.

The old school house was replaced by a new building in 1896. Land was purchased from Thomas Casey for five dollars. The new school building was erected next to the

Catholic cemetery. Miss Katherine Casey of Starksboro was the first teacher. With the passing years the population of Little Ireland became smaller and smaller. Finally, in 1944, the school was closed. In 1951 the building was sold for a summer camp. It is now owned by Mr. and Mrs. Ridley Norton of Bristol.

Submitted by
Bertha B. Hanson
1963 Town Report

*Little Ireland Schoolhouse, 1896.* **(34)**

The stream which runs through the present village of Starksboro was an ideal source of power for the development of the industries essential to a new settlement formed mostly by the confluent waters of three springs located not more than twenty rods apart. It flows swiftly down hill for a considerable distance.

John Ferguson, the first settler in the area now comprising Starksboro Village, owned a large tract of land extending on both sides of the stream and also the water privileges of the springs. He built the first grist mill in the town, now Amos Hanson's barn. Above this, he operated a saw mill. His forge, located on the hill east of the village, gave the name "Forge Hill" to the locality. He also owned the first fulling mill in town as well as a trip-hammer shop. In order to insure sufficient water for the operation of the industries along the stream, he "tunneled" through a small hill thus diverting the waters of the brook which flows from Brown Hill into the stream from the springs. At an early date, the Starksboro Aqueduct Company was formed to control this water power.

As the town grew, new industries sprung up. William Worth, writing about 1867, stated that there were in operation for many years a saw-mill, a fulling-mill, two forges, and two trip-hammer shops, all within a distance of little more than half a mile from the head of the stream. In 1819, Elisha Ferguson and Samuel Bushnell began the operation of a foundry on the farm now occupied by Leroy Smith. Later this was moved to a location west of Charles Thibault's store. For many years David Ferguson manufactured plows there. As early as 1848 reference was made to a starch factory located near the present residence of Mrs. Estelle Brownell. A tannery, which stood east of Rena Tobin's house, was operated by James Washburne & Sons. In 1831 George Ferguson began the manufacture of carriages and in 1868 the grist mill was remodeled for a carriage shop.

In the 1860's, Oscar D. Baldwin began the operation of the sawmill located near the present home of Robert Fuller. He also operated a stave-mill further down the stream. He did custom sawing, cooper work and owned a planing mill. Later he added a provender mill. In 1885 he employed two men in his sawmill. At that time he manufactured about 5,000 butter tubs and between 2,000 and 3,000 cheese boxes annually. These he stored in a building approximately 100 feet long and 40 feet wide. The large floor space made it an ideal place for an occasional dance or party. Mr. Baldwin also constructed a pond which he stocked with about 20,000 trout. The Agricultural yearbook, published in 1895, states that the largest of these weighed over a pound a piece.

Further up the stream near the present residence of Voda Brown, a fish hatchery operated for a number of years.

In the picture on the Town Report cover the buildings shown near the pond are those which were there when Oscar Baldwin owned the mills. A corner of the old Village school house which stood on the site now occupied by the Greta Knox house, can also be seen. The Knox house is shown connected with the house where Elbern Rublee now lives by a shed. The school house was removed in the later part of the nineteenth century and soon afterward the Knox house was moved to its present location.

Submitted by
Berth B. Hanson
1964 Town Report

*Baldwin Pond.*

***Baldwin's Mill.*** *Located above the village near the pond.*

***Baldwin's Mill.*** *Near the site of Bob Fuller's apartment house at the top of Village Hill.*

***Cooper/Livermore House. c. 1820.*** *This is an early house. The entry is unusual for the two almost full-sized windows flanking the door rather than the more common narrow sidelights. R.F. Livermore, a proprietor of the store next door, lived here in the 1870s. When it was the home of Fenwick and Paulita Estey, part of the house served as the Town's Post Office when Paulita was Postmaster. Now the home of Shawn & Katie O'Neil.* **(A6)**

***As Post Office,***
***1949-1972.*** **(A6)**

***Voda Brown House.*** *Now owned by Wayland and Leatha Brown.* **(15)**

***Jim Thompson - Voda Brown Place.*** *Now the property of Mr. and Mrs. Wayland Brown.* **(15)**

*Starksboro Village from the East, c.1900.*

*Livermore & Hill Store, c. 1850/Frank N. Hill House, c.1865. The left part of this building is exceptionally note-worthy as a rare and well-preserved example of a Greek Revival style store. Details to look at are the original c.1850 storefront windows, the paneled door, and the pilasters on the building corners. The store may have been established by Noble Boynton. Frank N. Hill began his business here in 1869. He and his partner, R.F. Livermore, were "Dealers in Dry Goods, Groceries, Hats and Caps, Hardware, Drugs and Medicines, Paints and Oils, Crockery, Boots and Shoes etc." Hill lived in the attached house, which may have been added in the late 1860s. Now the home of Ruby Craig. (A7)*

***House & Store Owned by Frank M. Hill.*** *Picture before 1912. L.to R. Laban Hill, Candace Hill, Kate (Chafee) Hill, Bertha Hill, Katie Hill, Sarah (Hill) Hill. Note Hitching Rail for Horses.* **(A7)**

***Village Street Scene Starksboro, Vt.*** **(A8** *on left)*

The section of Starksboro known as Shaker Hill was first settled about 1803. One of the earliest settlers was Aaron Blodgett who located near the "gully bridge".

At about the same time Hibbard Morrill, a Revolutionary War veteran from Barnstead, New Hampshire, settled on the place now owned by Ben Roberts. During the early years bears often "worked" in the settlers' corn fields doing a great deal of damage. Hibbard Morrill is said to have killed nineteen near his home. His son, Timothy, bought land on Shaker Hill in 1806. Two others sons, Isaac and Hibbard, Jr., settled there also.

In 1809 Ruth Eddy of Wallingford, Vermont, a widow with young sons, purchased a tract of land in the area. For many years, Caleb Eddy lived on the road leading to the Rindfusz place. His farm buildings, which were located a short distance from the turn, are now gone.

Moses Smith transported his goods by ox team from Barnstead, New Hampshire in the cold spring of 1816. Crops were poor that summer. It is said that the spring of 1817 found the family in such dire circumstances that he spent his last two dollars for a bushel of rye and gave two days work for the use of a team to transport it to the nearest mill to be ground. The old Moses Smith residence is now the home of Francis Craig. Alfred Smith, Moses' son, resided on the farm now owned by Marble Pierce.

In 1812 Joseph Beers purchased land from Aaron Blodgett. He was followed in 1813 by Ezekeil Ross from Wallingford, Vermont. Edmond Whittier arrived in 1817. Stephen Remington and Nathan Beers also came at an early date.

With increasing settlement the need for a school became apparent. On December 29, 1830 an Indenture was drawn up between Moses Smith and the Prudential Committee of the 6th School District of Starksboro, the members of which were Hibbard Morrill, Jr., Linus Rounds and Caleb Eddy. This agreement gave the committee and their successors in office the right to...'the land on which the house now stands built by Jesse Remington, Moses Smith, and Linus Rounds for a school house in said 6th district....in consideration of the value of one curnel of wheat to be paid to me yearly...." This building, which served Shaker Hill as long as there was need for a school, is now the home of Mary Marks.

Submitted by Bertha B. Hanson
1965 Town Report

***Moses Smith Place.*** *Long the residence of Francis Craig, it is now the property of his sons. Located on the corner by the Ben Roberts Road turn on Shaker Hill.*

***Shaker Hill Schoolhouse, c.1830.*** *Last used as a school in the early 1950s. Now owned by Craig family.* **(20)**

The first settlement in the Mason Hill area was probably made by Henry Tibbets, Jr. prior to 1810. His father, Henry, Sr. of Canterbury, N.H., purchased adjoining second division lots, numbers 67 and 70, in 1804. He deeded them to Henry, Jr. "of Starksboro" in 1810. These lots included the land where the school house and cemetery are now located. Henry, Jr. constructed buildings and made improvements on his property.

In 1809, Jonathan Gay, a young man from Starksboro Village, purchased the land now known as the Doland Place and owned by Dr. William Cardell of Bristol. Several members of the Gay family are said to have been buried on the farm but the tombstones cannot be located. This portion of the Mason Hill School District was long known as Gay Hill.

In 1812 Jethro Stokes from Northfield, New Hampshire moved his family to Starksboro. He purchased property at the height of land on the road which leads from the old Mason Hill school house to the Harley Brace residence. Here he built a house and cleared land for a farm. This farm was operated by his descendants until 1909.

Ebenezer Clifford came to Starksboro in 1813. He, too, was from Northfield, New Hampshire. His farm was located between the old school house and the Jethro Stokes property.

Soon Deacon David Mason of Northfield, New Hampshire, father-in-law of both Jethro Stokes and Ebenezer Clifford, decided to move his family to Starksboro. On October 31, 1817, he acquired the property which had been improved by Henry Tibbets, Jr. "with all the buildings thereon" for the sum of one thousand dollars. Later he bought more land in the area. He deeded property to his son, David, Jr., in 1822. In 1824 he deeded one hundred acres of land to his grandson, Benjamin Ellison, who had come to Vermont with him. For many years the Mason and Ellison families occupied portions of the old farm.

Greenleaf Ring, another early resident of Mason Hill, lived on the farm now known as the Chub Thompson place.

Mason Hill School House, built at an early date, served as a gathering place for the people of the district. Church services and funerals were held there. As early as 1816 Jonathan Gay served the town as a school trustee. It was not until March 6, 1832, however, that the boundaries for the various school districts in Starksboro were established. The Mason Hill District was described as follows: "Beginning at the Southwest corner of Lot. No. 71 in the 2nd Division Thence Northerly on the most extreme Lines around the following described Lots so as to include said Lots in said 8th School District..." The lots mentioned formed a rectangular group, all in the second Division, numbered 58, 59, 61-68, 70 and 71. Included within the district were farms on both the north and south sides of Gay Hill, those on Mason Hill, and several in the Big Hollow, as well as the so-called Pete Haskins place on the opposite hillside. These boundaries were retained by the Mason Hill School District until the school was closed in the late 1930's.

Bertha B. Hanson
1966 Town Report

**Walt Mason Farm.** *This place and property south was owned by the Masons. Then Cash Liberty bought both properties. W. Mason was David Mason's grandfather. Now home of Elliot Putnam and Linda Steinmiller on Big Hollow Rd.*

***The Will Ellison Place on Mason Hill South.*** *Original buildings are gone. Property belongs to Turner Brooks' Family.*

S haker Hill" received its name because of the association of one of the early settlers with the Shaker movement. Joseph Sanborn owned a prosperous farm in Canterbury, New Hampshire. In 1782, when Shakerism first began to gain momentum in that section, the entire family – Joseph, his wife, Deborah, and their three children – joined the group. Joseph soon became one of the leaders of the new faith. Those who attained full membership in the order were required to donate their property to the Shaker community to be administered for the common good of the group. The Sanborn farm, which became the home for probationary members who were being instructed and prepared for advancement in Shakerism, is now a part of Shaker Village, Canterbuy, New Hampshire.

After a few years Joseph Sanborn became dissatisfied with Shakerism. His wife and children, however, wished to remain with the community. In accordance with the regulations of the Shaker order a separation was mutually agreed upon and Joseph received a share of the property which he had previously donated to the order. He was then free, not only to manage his own affairs, but to re-marry if he wished.

Soon afterward, on May 22, 1800, Joseph Sanborn of Canterbury, New Hampshire, received a deed to the second division lot which had been drawn to the original right of John Stark in Starksboro, Vermont. He settled there and on April 6, 1801, married Eunice Tucker of Starksboro. Her family had also been associated with the Shaker movement. Soon the townspeople were referring to the section of town where the Sanborns lived as "Shaker Hill".

Joseph Sanborn died in 1803. The farm was then purchased by John Ferguson who immediately sold it to Hibbard Morrill. Ben and Elizabeth Roberts are the present owners. (Alan Roberts)

Nathan Sanborn, son of Joseph and Eunice, was for many years a merchant in Starksboro village.

Submitted by Bertha Hanson
1967 Town Report

***Hulett Place.*** *Now home of Alan Roberts. Located at end of Ben Roberts Rd.*

***Hulett Place.***
*Alan Robert's home.*

The "Rounds District" is located in the section of Starksboro which lies on the east side of Brown Hill overlooking Hanksville. In 1832, when the town was divided into school districts, eight Second Division Lots, Nos. 19-24, 53 and 54 were included in District No. 16.

Lot No. 24-2, located on the Huntington Town Line, was purchased by John Fitch, Jr. in 1824. On May 4, 1826 he sold it to James Haskins who was the first to make a permanent settlement in the district. Hibbard Morrill, Jr. bought Lot No. 20-2 in 1831. In November of that year Jesse Remington obtained the lease of Grammar School Lot No. 19-2. The Starksboro Selectmen leased Minister Lot No. 22-2 to Ephraim Brown in 1839. In 1840 James Haskins transferred to this son, Solon, the lease of University of Vermont Lot No. 21-2 which he had obtained in 1837. Elisha Rounds purchased a farm in the area in 1844. His family remained in the district for many years. Eventually District No. 16 became known as the "Rounds District".

Mary, wife of Aaron Brown, acquired a home site from James Haskins in 1830. The family lived there for several years. One afternoon while they were engaged in making soap, Mary and Aaron quarreled violently. Aaron disappeared. Several weeks passed and he did not return. Town officials, apprised of his disappearance by neighbors who had heard the quarrel, became alarmed and arrested Mary and her sister. They were charged with murdering Aaron and making him into soap. A Justice Court was set up to try the case. It convened in the hall above Asahel Wentworth's old tavern in Starksboro Village. An eyewitness describes the scene thus: "Aaron's wife and her sister were seated in two chairs near the table. Two Justices of the Peace were seated on the opposite side. There was a sap bucket full of bones under the table, and another containing about two gallons of soft soap sat near it..... The prisoners were clad in half worn calico dresses, the figure of which faded into the ground-work, giving the appearance of being stained with blood."

After a two day trial it was proven conclusively that, when Aaron and his wife were quarreling, she screamed at him, "You ought to be killed and made into soap!" Moreover, it was evident that Mary and her sister had made more soap than their available supply of grease warranted.

At the climax of the trial the town's only physician, the much respected Dr. Levered Clark, was called in to examine the bones which had already been proven to be those used in the manufacture of the soap. In the words of a spectator, "He carefully examined bone after bone, and at last laid aside two small bones which he said were human. He soon came to another large bone which he examined closely, and then, putting on his spectacles, he examined it very minutely for a long time. The right hand which held the bone commenced trembling violently, and the doctor seemed much agitated. He looked toward the prisoners and toward the court and said in a tremulous voice 'This is a piece of human skull....'"

The evidence was conclusive. The prisoners began to weep. The justices whispered together as they prepared their verdict.

Suddenly a shout was heard outside which grew louder as someone approached the hotel. Hurried footsteps sounded on the stairs; the door burst open. There stood a dark complexioned man of medium height – none other than Aaron Brown himself!

Thus ended Starksboro's first murder trial – the most exciting event in the long history of School District No. 16.

Submitted by Bertha Hanson
1968 Town Report

*Looking North from the Creamery, Starksboro.*

# 1969

The first Vermont Constitution, adopted in 1777, made the following provision for the election of town representatives: "The House of Representatives of the Freemen of this State should consist of Persons noted for Wisdom and Virtue, to be chosen by the Freemen of every town in this State respectively." The second constitution, adopted in 1786, contained much the same provisions. After Vermont joined the Union in 1791, it was thought advisable to re-write the constitution and in 1793 the third Vermont Constitution was adopted. It has continued in use until the present time with numerous amendments. Chapter 2, Section 13 states: "In order that the Freemen of the State may enjoy the benefit of election as equally as may be, each inhabited town in this State may, forever hereafter, hold elections therein and choose one Representative to represent them in the House of Representatives..."

The Vermont Legislature convened for the first time at Windsor in March, 1778. Until 1870 representatives were elected annually and the regular sessions of the Legislature convened each year, usually in October, for about thirty days. At that time an amendment calling for biennial elections became effective. The Legislature contin-ued to meet in October, but the sessions lengthened to about two or three months every other year. In 1913 another amendment was enacted which called for the General Assembly to convene on the first Wednesday after the first Monday of January, beginning in 1915. This gave the 1912-1913 Legislature an extra year – 1914 – in office.

In 1965 the system of town representation was abolished. A constitutional amendment was enacted which divided the state into districts, many of which included several towns. Starksboro became a part of District 61 composed of Hinesburg, Starksboro and Monkton. The first District Representative, Henry Carse, of Hinesburg, took office in 1966.

Town government was first organized in Starksboro in 1796. The town sent John Ferguson as the first Representative to the State Legislature in 1798. Prior to 1808 the Legislature had no established meeting place. Sessions were held annually in one of the larger towns. The Vermont Legislative Directory describes the situation thus: "Governors, Councilors, and Legislators were as peripatetic as German peddlers, and not infrequently footed their way, with packs of clothing and provisions on their backs." In 1808 the first State House, located in Montpelier, was ready for occupancy. Since that time the Legislature has met in Montpelier.

Between 1798 and 1807 the representatives from Starksboro traveled to the following towns for legislative sessions: 1798-Vergennes; 1799-Windsor; 1800-Middlebury; 1801-Newport; 1802-Burlington; 1803-Westminster; 1804-a session at Windsor in January and another at Rutland in October; 1805-Danville; 1806-Middlebury; 1807-Woodstock.

## Town Representatives
### 1798-1965

| Name | In Office | Born/Died | Name | In Office | Born/Died |
|------|-----------|-----------|------|-----------|-----------|
| John Ferguson | 1798-1804 | 1753-1815 | John Hill III | 1836 | 1799-1848 |
| Samuel Hill | 1805 | 1765-1843 | Ira Bushnell | 1837-1838 | 1799-1872 |
| John Ferguson | 1806 | 1753-1815 | Alman Atwood | 1839 | c.1792-1856 |
| Samuel Hill | 1807 | 1765-1843 | Benjamin Knight | 1840-1841 | c.1802 -1880 |
| John Ferguson | 1808-1809 | 1753-1815 | Theron J. Kidder | 1842 | |
| Elisha Ferguson | 1810 | 1780-1845 | Ansel S. Hawkins | 1843-1844 | 1808-1892 |
| Samuel Hill | 1811 | 1765-1843 | Isiah L. Strong | 1845-1846 | c.1812 -1880 |
| Elisha Ferguson | 1812-1814 | 1780-1845 | David Ferguson | 1847-1848 | c.1808-1895 |
| Ezekiel Pease | 1815 | c.1756-1837 | Pearley Hill | 1849-1850 | 1804-1876 |
| Elisha Ferguson | 1816-1818 | 1780-1845 | Samuel D. Holcomb | 1851 | 1807-1880 |
| Ebenezer Blodget | 1819 | | Sidney Sayles | 1852 | c.1800-1878 |
| David Kellogg | 1820 | c.1766-1850 | George W. Ferguson | 1854-1855 | c.1813-1889 |
| Elisha Ferguson | 1821-1823 | 1780-1845 | Lee Taft | 1856-1857 | c.1821 |
| Myron Bushnell | 1824-1825 | 1791 -c1887 | Charles M. H. Ferguson | 1858-1859 | c.1816 1894 |
| Elijah Ferguson | 1826 | 1775-1850 | Cyrus W. Atwood | 1860-1861 | 1817-1891 |
| Elijah Ferguson | 1827 | 1775-1850 | Joel Orvis | 1862-1863 | 1813-1902 |
| Myron Bushnell | 1828 | 1791- c.1887 | Thomas Morrison | 1864-1865 | 1831-1890 |
| Asahel Wentworth | 1829 | c.1789-1833 | Franklin N. Hill | 1866-1867 | 1820-1904 |
| Myron Bushnell | 1830-1831 | 1791-c.1887 | Edwin W. Washburn | 1868-1869 | 1830 |
| Theron Downey | 1832-1833 | c.1801-1881 | Albert Orvis | 1870-1871 | 1834-1922 |
| William Worth II | 1834-1835 | c.1799-1881 | Rollin M. Livermore | 1872-1873 | 1843-1893 |

| Name | In Office | Born/Died | Name | In Office | Born/Died |
|------|-----------|-----------|------|-----------|-----------|
| Burritt J. Grennell | 1874-1875 | 1844-c.1917 | John W. Dike | 1917-1918 | 1869-1963 |
| Sidney Bushnell | 1876-1877 | 1838-1920 | Walter W. Mason | 1919-1920 | 1864-1962 |
| Josiah G. Fuller | 1878-1879 | 1839-1910 | Jesse Carpenter | 1921-1922 | 1875-1955 |
| Joseph Sylvester Hill | 1880-1881 | 1824-1894 | Daniel H. Sargent | 1923-1924 | 1868-1933 |
| Joel Willis Orvis | 1882-1883 | 1856-1936 | George G. Elliott | 1925-1926 | 1873-1937 |
| Wallace N. Hill | 1884-1885 | 1843-1925 | Andrew I. Hallock | 1927-1928 | 1885-1958 |
| Edgar J. Purinton | 1886-1887 | 1847-1897 | James P. Conway | 1929-1930 | 1868-1929 |
| Charles L. Atwood | 1888-1889 | 1848-1932 | Clinton F. Smith | 1931-1932 | 1883-1961 |
| Joel V. Carpenter | 1890-1891 | 1845-1907 | Vesper C. Thompson | 1933-1934 | 1883-1936 |
| Henry Wade, M.D. | 1892-1893 | 1852-1933 | Russell D. Young | 1935-1936 | 1896 |
| Calvin F. Clifford | 1894-1895 | 1853-1938 | Edgar W. Smith | 1937-1938 | 1888-1954 |
| Leslie George Ferguson | 1896-1897 | 1854-1920 | Henry S. Hallock | 1939-1940 | 1887-1960 |
| Daniel H. Orvis | 1898-1899 | 1842-1922 | Floyd F. Smith | 1941-1942 | 1887-1966 |
| Frank M. Hill | 1900-1901 | 1858-1950 | Ernest K. Eddy | 1943-1946 | 1879-1962 |
| Warren B. Thompson | 1902-1903 | 1844 -c.1904 | Clarence C.Atwood | 1947-1948 | 1894-1953 |
| George E. O'Brien | 1904-1905 | 1856-1939 | Calvin E. Moore | 1949-1950 | 1902 |
| Walter Baldwin | 1906-1907 | 1870-1930 | Gale B. Mason | 1951-1954 | 1897-1966 |
| Bial C. Fuller | 1908-1909 | 1875-1947 | William C. Knox | 1955-1958 | 1879-1963 |
| Milo Wright | 1910-1911 | 1857-1929 | Floyd Frank Smith | 1959-1960 | 1887-1966 |
| Wilson Briggs | 1912-1914 | 1856-1920 | Walter Chase Stokes | 1961-1962 | 1902 |
| Walter E. Smith | 1915-1916 | 1876-1928 | Robert M. Thompson | 1963-1965 | 1920 |

## Addison County Senators
## From Starksboro

| Name | Years in Office | Born/Died |
|------|-----------------|-----------|
| Samuel D Holcomb | 1862-1863 | 1807-1880 |
| Wallace N. Hill | 1900-1902 | 1843-1925 |

Several men who represented Starksboro in the State Legislature later moved to other states. Myron Bushnell died in Guernsey, Iowa; Theron Downey in Brandon, Wisconsin; Thomas Morrison in Chicago, Ilinois; Joel Willis Orivis in Denver, Colorado; Charles Leslie Atwood in Long Beach, California; Frank M. Hill in York, Maine; and Alman Atwood was lost in the burning of a steamer on Lake Michigan.

Submitted by Bertha B. Hanson
1969 Town Report

On January 26, 1898 Articles of Association of the Green Mountain Cold Spring Creamery were filed in the office of the Secretary of State by Frank M. Hill, David Bostwick, Isaac Harris, George O'Bryan, Calvin Clifford and Almon L. White. These articles stated, "We, the subscribers hereby associate ourselves together as a Corporation under the Laws of the State of Vermont to be known by the name of the Green Mountain Cold Spring Creamery for the purpose of manufacturing butter and buying, selling and dealing generally in milk and milk products and doing all things incident thereto and connected therewith at Starksboro in the County of Addison in the State of Vermont, with a Capital Stock of Fifteen Hundred Dollars divided into one hundred and fifty shares of Ten Dollars each." Three days later Isaac Harris gave the corporation a lease of a piece of land east of the highway running through Starksboro Village for "as long as it shall be occupied for creamery purposes or the manufacture of dairy products". In the Fall of 1899 rights to a spring located on the Isaac Harris property were obtained from Maranda Swift. Local farmers bought shares of stock in the new creamery. They separated their milk at home and fed the skim milk to hogs and calves. Since the creamery used only sour cream in the manufacture of butter, cream kept satisfactorily in cans in the farm water box for several days. Most farmers planned to "go to the creamery" every other day in summer and every third day in winter but a few went only once a week. Farmers who raised hogs for market often supplemented their supply of skim milk with buttermilk from the creamery. The new enterprise prospered, and in 1907 the corporation bought the house now owned by Robert Merrill, Senior (Bryan Merrill in 1997) as a residence for the butter maker.

Green Mountain Cold Spring Creamery continued to operate until 1916 when David Donahue and W. C. Donahue of Monkton of Monkton purchased the plant for $4,000. On May 14, 1918 the Donahues sold the business to the newly organized Starksboro Farmers' Cooperative Association, Inc. for $5,000. The incorporators were Wallace N. Hill, N. John Maxfield, Jesse L. Carpenter, N. L. Thompson, John W. Dike, W. D. Walden, Arthur E. Clifford and J. W. Corey. The corporation issued 500 shares of stock at $10 each. Each shareholder was allowed one vote, and no shareholder could own more then $500 worth of stock. The creamery continued to buy cream and make butter, but

*Green Mountain Cold Spring Creamery, 1898/c.1910.* Built in the 1890s the creamery at this time was still handling cream and making butter. **(A1)**

changing economic conditions and increasing problems of operation finally resulted in the decision to sell the business. On March 2, 1928 Fred O. Brown, as duly authorized agent, deeded the plant to D.E. Hinman and George Polley. Hinman and Polley bought from Frank and Lois Harris the land previously leased to the creamery by Isaac Harris. Shortly thereafter the business became the property of the Monkton Creamery Company, Inc.

With the increased use of trucks for transportation, markets in the large industrial cities of southern New England became accessible to farmers in northern Vermont. It became profitable to ship fluid milk to Boston. Silverman Brothers purchase the Starksboro Creamery in the summer of 1928 and in 1929 began to process whole milk.

In 1935 Albert J. Robinson of Boston acquired the creamery property. Under his direction the plant, which he named Mountain View Creamery, again became a successful business enterprise. He enlarged the building and installed new equipment. In 1936 he bought a large spring east of the village and piped the water to the creamery. The following year he purchased additional land on the west side of the highway. In 1942, since the house belonging to the creamery property had previously been sold, he purchased the dwelling directly south of the creamery as a residence for the manager.

As the years passed, Mountain View Creamery acquired new patrons from other towns. Monkton, Bristol, Lincoln, New Haven, Huntington and Williston were represented. Some farmers brought their milk to the plant themselves; others hired it trucked. The milk was processed at the Starksboro plant, transferred to large tank trucks and shipped to Boston for fluid consumption. In 1953, when farmers began installing bulk tanks, the creamery purchased a bulk truck to haul milk directly from the farmers to the plant. This proved so practical that in 1963 they demanded that all farmers shipping to the plant convert to bulk milk.

The creamery continued under the ownership of A.J. Robinson, and later that of his son Dexter Robinson, until 1966. It was then reorganized as Mountain View Creamery, Inc. under the direction of Lloyd Stearns who had come to Starksboro as a manager in 1946.

In 1970 Mountain View Creamery, Inc. came under the operation of Needham Dairies, Inc. of Needham, Massachuetts.

Bertha B. Hanson
1970 Town Report

(*The 1971 Town Report was an Autobiography by Ben Roberts which we are quite sure was reviewed and/or edited by Bertha B. Hanson.*)

## Autobiography

If you think that the picture on the cover of this report looks like me – I am sorry, either because of your opinion, or because it may be true. Truth, I have discovered, is not always pleasant.

It was suggested that something about me and my life (thus far) might be printed on this page. Immediately I begged permission to do the writing of this "epitaph" – simply for safety's sake, of course. Heaven knows how it may be edited. I like to call it a happy and somewhat uneventful life, which, by no means, I can think of, can I puff up into importance. When I read the long columns of print beneath the pictures of some folks as they appear in public press I often feel chagrined. What a short list could I come up with in comparison! Yet I wonder also (sometimes) if such lists are always as significant as news reporters would seem to indicate. At any rate mine is as follows.

In 1891 I was born in a then tiny place called Wayne, Pa., near Philadelphia, where my father taught Latin and Greek in the fa-

mous Penn Charter School. When I was nine we moved to Brookline, Mass., where I attended both Grammar and High Schools, and managed to graduate from both. The kindliest act of Heaven caused me to meet a lovely, blue-eyed girl – yes, even in grammar school – and we have stuck together ever since. There are utterly immeasurable gifts of Providence - often surprisingly bestowed.

In High School I had my father for a Latin teacher – rough on me, even rougher on him. He had one son who was a good scholar, and a young daughter who was a "whiz". I was in the middle – a double disappointment – I was supposed to be a girl – and sure wasn't – I was supposed to be above average as a student – and while I "got by", I sometimes barely skidded through. Alas, I told my father, I did not want to go to college – too much like steady book work. "Young man", he replied to me, "don't think that I have saved money every month since you were born (which was true) to pay for your college education and make you go. "But", and here he had me where the hair was short, "you ARE going to pass the examinations."

This was what I had chiefly hoped to avoid. Yet I had a horror of the disgrace that might fall upon the family if I failed the exams. So it came to pass that I <u>did</u> go to college after all. My father (not the government) paid the bills save for a few dollars I earned working with my hands in summer. And I graduated from Harvard in 1913.

I am not going to discuss the questions as to how it happened that I then went on to the theological school, Andover Theological Seminar, from which I graduated with the startling degree of Bachelor of Theology in 1916. The reasons seemed sound to me then, and I trust they were.

My ordination to the ministry in the Congregational Church followed. The little blue-eyed girl who, for unbelievable reasons, had been waiting for me and teaching school for three years until I should get my degree, married me the day after it was bestowed. We settled in Ashburnham, Mass., where Cushman Academy is located. In those days, students were required to attend some church – and many happened to come to mine. There I swiftly learned the futility of dull preaching. Teenagers, even in those days, developed methods of making their opinions apparent. They taught me much. I hope there may have been some reciprocity here. I am not certain.

Twin boys arrived in our household – and problems, of course, but we all came through – and when the babies were two and a half years old we moved to Proctor, Vermont – the Union Church – where we lived for almost ten years. There our daughter was born. Then back we went to Massachusetts to what was our main parish, lasting seventeen years, in Newton Highlands Congregational Church.

A suburban church of more than eight hundred members tends to exhaust a minister's time and energy – if he honestly tries to do his real jobs (definitions here are debatable today). The Second World War came, was fought, and supposedly was ended. Our longing grew for the wide ocean, the deep woods and the mountains – something atavistic in both of us. The war was over, our three youngsters had done their duty and were "on their own". We had long had a camp at Lake Dunmore, but when there were no children in it and houses were coming close in, we took to hiking most of the length of the Long Trail. Then the blue-eyed girl tripped over a rock near Killington's top – and we spent the rest of our vacation in our car knocking about back roads in Vermont – for her plaster cast arm prohibited hiking.

So by the sheerest accident we chanced upon the Hulett Farm – for sale. The blue-eyed girl who had never once asked me for anything for herself said, "I want it". So she got it – and you got us.

Starksboro had now been our home for more than twenty-five years – longer than anywhere else. We are fond of the place and people. The Town's populace is changing – and is inevitable – but the eternal hills are there. They do not change (much). To have been trusted with the Moderator's gavel these many years is an honor I shall never forget. We have had some grand fights in Town Meeting. Far better than a silent acquiescence – often an indication of indifference, or fear. I, personally, have always been treated with courtesy – even a surprisingly friendly appreciation. I shall still be "around" – at least for a while. It may well happen that I shall be ruled "out of order" as I have ruled others. I have banged the gavel for the last time, I suppose – but thank God – we live in a country where free men continue to hand a gavel to some one of them that order and fair play shall prevail.

Ben Roberts
1971 Town Report

# 1972

At the Annual Town Meeting held in March, 1941, Ila H. Smith was elected Town Clerk and Treasurer. On March 7 of that year Leroy and Ila Smith purchased from Amos Hanson a small building, which was then being used as a garage, together with the land on which it set, for the sum of $75. This they remodeled for use as a Town Clerk's Office.

Previous to this time there had been no office for the Town Clerk. In the early years of the town the clerk kept the books in his own home and did his work there.

When Ansel M. Hawkins, the towns' first attorney, became Town Clerk in 1869 he moved the books into his law office, a building which also served as the post office during the years in which he was postmaster. Mr. Hawkins purchased the property where John and Colleen Whitten now reside, in 1835. Near his north line, on the road then leading west to the Ferguson and Wentworth Forge, he built a small building for use as an office. This building, sold to Arland Smith about 1918, was moved across the road and placed on land purchased from Charles N. Bickford. It was the same building purchased in 1941 by Leroy and Ila Smith for use as a Town Clerk's Office.

In 1883 Charles Leslie Atwood, propri-etor of the store which is now operated by Charles and Margaret Thibault (Andrew & Cheryl Young in 1997), became Town Clerk. The books were then moved into his store. Leslie G. Ferguson, who purchased the store from him, was also his successor as Town Clerk. Therefore the books continued to be kept in the store until the present Town Hall was completed in 1911 and a safe installed there for the protection of the town records. Frank S. Ferguson, Town Clerk 1915-1921, also owned and operated the store and much of the actual work of the Town Clerk continued to be done there though the records were kept in the Town Hall. Anna Ferguson, Jane Bickford, and Rena Tobin did most of their work in their homes using the safes in the Town Hall for the safe keeping of record books and papers.

When Leroy and Ila Smith purchased the "Old Town Clerk's Office" the safes were moved from the Town Hall into this building. It was furnished as an office and most of the work of the clerk and treasurer was done there.

Ila Smith decided not to run for Town Clerk in 1947. Her successor, Oliver Besaw, continued to use the building, however. On May 12, 1949, when Ruby B. Craig was serving as Town Clerk, the town purchased the building and the land on which it set from Leroy and Ila Smith for $150 for use as Town Clerk's Office. It served this purpose until 1973 when the new Town Clerk's Office, built on adjoining land given to the town by Leroy and Ila Smith, was completed and opened for use.

Bertha B. Hanson & Ila H. Smith
1972 Town Report

***Union Store, c. 1860.*** *This is the second store located on this site. An earlier one deeded to Samuel Bushnell in 1805 burned. This one, called the Union Store on the 1871 map, was run for years by Cyrus W. Atwood who began business in 1868. His son and successor, Charles Leslie Atwood, was a watchmaker and jeweler who later moved to Burlington and then to Long Beach, CA. He and the following storekeepers, Leslie G. and Frank S. Ferguson, also town clerks, kept the town books here from 1883 until 1911 when the Town Hall was built. The post office was also here until the early 1930s. The second floor was added c. 1900. The garage section may have been a blacksmith shop. Presently the Starksboro Village Store owned by Cheryl and Andy Young.* **(A34)**

Most of the early settlers of South Starksboro were members of the Religious Society of Friends. When a sufficient number of Quakers had moved into a locality they requested the privilege of holding an "allowed" meeting for worship from the nearest monthly meeting. In 1799 the Lincoln-South Starksboro area, which formed a geographic entity served by the road known as Quaker Street, was granted by the Danby (Vt.) Monthly Meeting, begun in 1809, "12th da. 3rd mo. 1815". Starksborough Monthly Meeting, made up of Lincoln Meeting, Montpelier Meeting, and the Quaker Meeting north of Starksboro Village received the following letter: "Beloved Friends, We have taken into consideration a proposition for holding a meeting for worship in our neighborhood and in weighing the matter we believe it right to request your advice and assistance in the case." Twenty-two people signed this request. Starksborough Monthly Meeting united in allowing a meeting "on first and fifth days at the eleventh hour at the home of David Morrison." In 1825 this meeting was established as "a meeting for worship and preparative meeting in the south part of Starksborough...by the name of Creek Meeting."

Friends of Creek Meeting submitted to Starksborough Monthly Meeting a proposal for purchasing one acre of land from Philander Orvis and a half acre from David Morrison "for the purpose of a burying ground and to set a meeting house on." The land deeded "24th da. 4th mo. 1826", cost $18.30. A building 34 feet in length and 26 feet in width was decided upon, the estimated cost of which was $360. Eliphalet Johnson, Asa Chase, Philander Orvis and Moses Sargent were appointed to superintend the construction. On "2nd da. 5th mo. 1828" Stephen Green was granted a request for "a meeting appointed at Creek Meeting House at one o'clock tomorrow" ....for his wedding.

The census of Friends completed about 1828 by the New York Yearly Meeting of the Society of Friends listed membership of Creek Meeting as 70. All children born into a Quaker family are birthright members of the society.

In 1832 the Starksborough Monthly Meeting insisted that the meeting house property be reduced in size. They suggested that 8 rods from the south acre be sold to the former owner, Philander Orvis for $6 and 4 rods of the north half acre be deeded back to David Morrison for $4.

*South Starksboro Friends Meeting House, 1826/1871.* Oldest place of continual Quaker worship in Vt. **(37)**

David Morrison refused to accept a deed so the 4 rod strip was deeded to George Harkness who later sold it to David Morrison's sons.

By the middle of the nineteenth century many Friends had moved to western New York and Iowa. The Starksborough Monthly Meeting was "laid down" and the members allocated to the Monkton Meeting. In 1851 Friends in the South Starksboro - Lincoln area forwarded the following request to the Ferrisburg Monthly meeting: "Since our meeting had been laid down we feel the want of a meeting. We therefore respectfully ask for a meeting for worship under your care . . . " A meeting was allowed to be held on first day at Creek and fifth day at Lincoln. It was known as Lincoln Preparative Meeting until 1881 when the name was changed to South Starksboro Preparative Meeting.

In 1871 the Creek Meeting House was remodeled. About 7 feet were added to the length and about 3-1/2 feet to the width. The whole project cost about $1,000. Even then the building was not large enough to accommodate the crowd at Quarterly Meetings. On those occasions the northeast window was removed and a door propped up outside to form a platform so that the minister could speak to those who had assembled both inside and outside the building.

Friends meetings experienced many changes toward the close of the nineteenth century. Music, long banned from worship services, became not only acceptable, but desirable. An organ was installed in the South Starksboro Meeting House much against the wishes of some of the older members. When the organ was played one elderly Quaker always went outside and sat on the board fence until the music stopped, then he returned to meeting. The traditional "unprogrammed" meeting was replaced by a service conducted by a minister. Levinus K. Painter, the last resident pastor, left South Starksboro about 1923. At present, services are held occasionally during the summer. They are usually "unprogrammed".

Notable among Quakers who grew up in South Starksboro was Thomas C. Battey. Born there in 1828, he spent many years as a school master among the Indians in the west. His book, entitled *Adventures of a Quaker Among the Indians*, is quoted in the best seller *Bury My Heart at Wounded Knee*. The brothers, Stephen and Joseph Green, became well known doctors. Dr. Joseph Green had the Lord's Prayer engraved on the Lord's Prayer Rock in Bristol.

The South Starksboro Friends Meeting House is the oldest, and with the exception of Monkton which now serves a United Congregation, the only Quaker Meeting House remaining in Vermont built by any of the state's once numerous Quaker Meetings which formed a constituent part of the New York Yearly Meeting of the Society of Friends.

Bertha B. Hanson
1973 Town Report

The earliest school record in Starksboro, a census of families with school age children taken in 1805, lists 61 families with 185 children. "School age" then applied to children of four or five who might be sent to school for the summer term only and also to the "big boys" in their middle teens who were able to attend only during the winter term when work at home was slack.

The first recorded Town Meeting minutes, those for March 29, 1808, refer to the establishment of School Districts "as followeth: All Southerly from Henry Chases to be in a District by the name of the fourth District, Hillsboro inhabitants all easterly of the Middle and North Districts to be known by the name of the Sixth School District."

The Middle District doubtless comprised the area within walking distance of Starksboro Village where the "Center School House," stood. Sometimes referred to as "the school house near Elisha Ferguson's," it was built on land first owned by John Ferguson and later by his son, Elisha. It stood on the spot where Greta Knox's house is now located.

The town grew rapidly. The school record of March 1, 1816, the date at which the school population reached its all time high, reads: "Scholars numbered and found to be 382 Scholars..."

At the 1832 Town Meeting the Town was divided into 17 School Districts. The First District, comprising the area around the Village, was described thus "Beginning at the northeast corner of Lot No. 60 in the first Division of Land set off from Monkton to Starksboro thence Westerly the most extreme line around the following described lots of land to the place of beginning so as to contain said lots in the first School District to wit: Lots 60-47-48-35 & 36 in the 1st Division and No. 14 in the 2nd Division of land set off from Monkton to Starksboro also of land in the old chartered bounds of said Starksboro Lots 2-3-4-5-6-7 & 8 in the first Division and also 1-2-3-4-5 & 6 in the 2nd Division.

The old Village School House, served the district well. Eventually, however, it was sold and moved to the place now owned by Ava Strong. It was used for a hen house until a few years ago when it was burned by the Starksboro Fire Department.

During the latter part of the nineteenth century townspeople began to feel that a new, larger, more impressive school building should be constructed in Starksboro Village. On April 27, 1892, the Town acquired a

***Beech Glen School.*** *Near Ruby Brace's on the northern end of Big Hollow Road, this little school house stood on the site where Maurice Brace is presently building his new house. (Now the home of Garry Jones.)*

deed from Page Smith to a half acre of land adjoining the Baptist Parsonage lot. There, a one-room schoolhouse of Victorian design was constructed.

A singing school often met there on winter evenings. A favorite trick of mischievous school boys was to turn the lamp wicks out of the burners and down into the oil during the afternoon preceding an evening gathering. It was even more fun to hide the key so early arrivals would have to climb through a window.

The number of students attending the village school varied over the years. At times forty or more pupils were enrolled in eight grades. In later years, as the population in the hill sections of the town declined, schools were closed and the students transported to the Village. At one time pupils from Hillsboro came to school in winter in a horse drawn covered sled heated by a wood burning stove.

In 1941 the old Village School was remodeled and enlarged. The resulting structure, containing two upstairs classrooms and hot lunch facilities in the basement, was named Robinson School in honor of Albert J. Robinson. Then owner of Mountain View

Creamery, he donated the necessary funds for the project.

The playground was enlarged in 1964 by the purchase of about two acres of land from Harold and Emma Shivarette.

In the fall of 1968 Mt. Abraham Union High School opened its doors to grades 7-12. Elementary pupils from South Starksboro were then transported to the Village School. For the first time all Starksboro Grade School students were housed under one roof. The town had become one School District.

Bertha B. Hanson
1974 Town Report

*The Gore Schoolhouse, c.1832/1904. Owned by William Gale.* **(23)**

"Oh, Jerusalem! You ain't so big as I thought you were," exclaimed an early resident of South Starksboro who, after climbing a hill near his home, turned to look across the valley where a small industrial community was growing up along the banks of Baldwin Creek in School District No. 15. Thus it was, remembers Elizabeth Birdsall Young, that "Jerusalem," the old man's favorite by-word, became the name by which the hamlet was thereafter known.

School District 15 was set off by vote of the town on April 14, 1827. Altered in 1832 when all Town School District boundaries were established, it was enlarged by the addition of four lots from District No. 4 in 1839.

The school house was built on private property – a common practice at that time – on the site of the present structure. "The School Lot; a part of Lot 59, the so-called Farnham Lot", was first mentioned in property boundaries given in a deed from Theodore Stearns to Major Rutherford on November 25, 1850.

At about this time land across the road was set aside for a burying ground. A short distance above on Baldwin Creek a saw mill was located on "Houston's Mill Pond." Soon shingle mills, clapboard and stave mills were established further up the stream. Blacksmith shops did a thriving business. A hotel served for traveling public. Jerusalem boasted a store where the South Starksboro Post Office, established in 1857, was located for many years. The South Starksboro Free Will Baptist Church was organized on Feb. 27, 1874.

That year the residents of District No. 15 built a new school house. Constructed on the site of the earlier building, it was designed to serve both as a church and a school. The structure, which would accommodate 75 pupils was, at the time, the largest and most impressive school house in town. A bell, mounted on the roof, called the people to worship on Sundays and the students to their studies on week days. On a plaque above the window in the gable end facing the road can still be discerned the words "School District No. 15, 1874" painted in fancy letters. Horse sheds were built to accommodate teams driven to church.

The Huntington Free Will Baptist Quarterly Meeting Conference met in Jerusalem September 4-6, 1874. Teams from far and near lined the highway on both sides of the school house. The little community had to provide food and lodging for visitors from

*Jerusalem School, 1874/1904.* **(31)**

as far away as Waterbury. Minutes of the meetings state, "The business of the conference was transacted with harmony and dispatch, giving ample room for prayer meetings, which were of most interesting character."

The South Starksboro Free Will Baptist Church disbanded in 1882. Members united with the Lincoln Church and with the First Baptist Church in Starksboro Village.

Thereafter *The Bristol Herald* carried frequent news of Sunday afternoon services at Jerusalem School conducted by Rev. John True Hill, of Lincoln, a Free Will Baptist Minister and the beloved Uncle True of many

South Starksboro residents. Former students still recall days when school was dismissed so that the school house could be used for afternoon funeral services.

In 1904 the building was remodeled. A new floor, new ceiling and new seats were installed. It was the proud boast of the South Starksboro reporter for *The Bristol Herald* that though "...no repairs of any extent have ever been made on it until now...when finished it will rank fairly well with any school house in town."

At one time 65 students attended Jerusalem School. The late Robert Young recalled the days when, as a student, he started the old wood stove for 5 cents a morning – $3 a term. Before her marriage his wife, the former Elizabeth Birdsall, taught there for $6.50 a week.

Levinus K. Painter, last resident pastor of the South Starksboro and Monkton Ridge Friends Meetings, included in his intensive ministry during the years 1921 to 1926 "...an informal Sunday evening meeting at Jerusalem School which is really at the center of the South Starksboro Community. For this evening service men came directly from their dairy barns bringing their lanterns for light and providing the distinct "aroma of the cow barns" for atmosphere...Usually the school house was well filled and on summer evenings there was lingering outside for neighborly conversation." For many years thereafter dedicated ladies from the community continued to hold Sunday School there.

In the early 1930s the South Starksboro Home Circle, anxious to improve the school building, presented plays in the school house and also in neighboring towns to raise money for the installation of a stage. Men from the neighborhood did the carpenter work. As a result the Home Circle was granted a 99-year lease by the Starksboro voters at Town Meeting in 1933.

On August 25, 1941, Milton Elliott deeded a piece of land adjoining the school lot to the town. The deed stated, "It is part of the consideration of this conveyance that the School House property may be used for

*Jerusalem School.*

72

community gatherings, for church or Sunday School, and at times when the same does not interfere with the regular school work."

Soon after this a small addition was built on the back of the building to accommodate a furnace, kitchen and bathroom facilities.

During its last years of operation the one room school at Jerusalem served Jerusalem, the West School and the Gore Districts.

Lucy Wyman, the last teacher to keep school there, completed her work in June, 1968. That fall, when Mt. Abraham Union High School opened, Jerusalem School was closed. Students from grades 1-6 were transported to Robinson School in Starksboro Village.

Jerusalem School, no longer needed for school purposes, became a community center for South Starksboro. A Community Club was organized which has since helped with the maintenance and upkeep of the building.

Bertha B. Hanson
1975 Town Report

# 1976

Starksboro's Official Bicentennial Week was celebrated June 13 through June 20, 1976. It was a meaningful and memorable time which began with a Worship Service on Sunday, June 13 at the First Baptist Church. Reverend Robert H. Martens delivered an inspiring sermon on "The Greatness of America". The guest soloist, Kenneth Dahlberg of Monkton, sang "The Vacant Chair" and Harold Gardner recited the Declaration of Independence. A special anthem, "A Nation's Praise and Prayer," was sung by the church choir, and organist Alice Russell led the congregation in the singing of patriotic hymns. The Scripture from I Peter 2:11-17 was read by Lars Gilbertson. At this service the Fireman were present, in their uniforms, together with the Auxiliary.

A flag presentation ceremony took place on the church lawn after the worship service. An American Flag which flew over the U.S. Capitol Building on May 20 was presented to the First Baptist Church. The Bicentennial Flag awarded the Town by the American Revolution Bicentennial Administration was also presented at this time. Representative Douglas Baker of District A-2 presented the American Flag to Harold Gardner, Chairman of the First Baptist Church, Inc. The Bicentennial Flag was presented by Mr. Baker to Bertha Hanson, Chairman of the Starksboro Bicentennial Committee, and by her to Ruford Brace, Selectman, who accepted it on behalf of the Town. The members of the Fire Department who, under the direction of Fire Chief Fenwick Estey, assisted in raising the flags were Leroy Smith, Retired Chief; Arthur Cota, 1st Assistant Chief; and David Estey, 2nd Assistant Chief. As the flags were raised, the audience, led by Kenneth Dahlberg, sang "The Star Spangled Banner". Fenwick Estey led the Flag Salute and the program closed with a solo, "God Bless America" by Mr. Dahlberg.

At noon the Volunteer Fire Department and the Women's Auxiliary served a turkey dinner at the Town Hall.

In the afternoon at 2:30 the dedication of the Town Municipal Building and the new Post Office Building took place on the Municipal Lot. A hay wagon, loaned by Wayne Hill for use as a platform, was decorated with white crepe paper and red, white and blue streamers by Thelma Bedard, Town Clerk, and her husband, Harold. The Town Moderator, Arthur Clifford, was Master of Ceremonies.

Hervey Hanson, great-great-grandson

of George Bidwell, first settler in 1787 of Starksboro as chartered, was introduced by the Bicentennial Chairman, Bertha Hanson. Mrs. Hanson also spoke of Samuel Stokes, a great-great-grandson of John Ferguson who settled about 1787 in the part of Starksboro Village originally included within the charter limits of Monkton. Mr. Stokes was unable to be present because of poor health.

Mrs. Thelma Bedard, Town Clerk and Treasurer, and Mrs. Barbara Bissonette of Hinesburg, Starksboro Postmaster, were introduced. Mr. Leon Andrus, Postmaster of Wolcott, Vermont, and Secretary-Treasurer for the Vermont Chapter of the National Association of Postmasters, gave a brief talk as a visitor from the postal services.

The speaker, Dr. T. Seymour Bassett of the University of Vermont, spoke about the changing relationship of government to the people in the years since our nation was founded. He emphasized the significance the two new buildings represented – the local government on one side of the Lot, the Federal government on the other – and yet standing together. The Bristol Middle School Band rendered several musical selections.

The Invocation was given by Reverend Robert H. Martens of the First Baptist Church and the Benediction by Reverend Basil Nichols, pastor of St. Ambrose Parish of Bristol.

On Sunday evening at 7 o'clock the choir from St. Ambrose Catholic Church in Bristol, directed by Sheila Lathrop, gave an outstanding program at the Starksboro Village Meeting House.

Throughout the day exhibits of crafts, antiques and family treasures were on view on the second floor at the Town Hall. The exhibits, sponsored by the Friendship Homemakers and organized by Mrs. Sue Jagels, Chairman of the Exhibit committee, emphasized the theme "Starksboro Then and Now." It included old farm tools, letters, family photographs, hand woven articles from by-gone days, quilts, old and new painting and handicraft of all kinds and a great variety of other small items. Edward Hannan and Richard Jagels demonstrated shingle making on the stage throughout the afternoon. A quilt made by Mrs. Susan Hanson's mother, Mrs. Herbert Lovell of Longview, Texas, was tied by the Home Demonstration Club. Sue Jagels demonstrated spinning. Mrs. Emma Shivarette, dressed in a Victorian costume with "mutton leg" sleeves, sewed on a one-threaded sewing machine. She also exhibited the old pattern designs she used in making the pattern for the dress.

The collection made by the Bicentennial Committee consisting of about 150 old pictures of houses, public buildings and industries in Starksboro, was on display.

The exhibits generated great interest and inspiration among residents and visitors alike and continued for four days during the Bicentennial Week.

On Monday night a community potluck supper was held at the Town Hall. Friends and neighbors enjoyed the good cooking and each other's company. Historic slides of the town's old buildings were shown as Bertha Hanson very interestingly described the history of these buildings and their owners through the years. An amusing feature was also presented by the Starksboro Public Library, – the showing of two old time movies, a silent Slapstick Comedy and a Laurel & Hardy movie.

On Wednesday, June 16, the Christian Culture Club sponsored a sale of home cooked food in the Church Vestry.

In the afternoon, the Vermont Bicentennial Bandwagon arrived at the Robinson Elementary School grounds in Starksboro. The Reverend Robert Martens and Robert Hall, as Masters of Ceremonies, announced the evening's activities.

The Robinson School children performed skits and the 6th grade class graduation took place on the Bandwagon stage. The members of the graduating class were Patsy Bedell, Jeffrey Fellows, Marie Fellows, Robin Fleming, Sara Gagnon, John Kamencik, James Orvis, Joseph Parent, Jacqueline Pechie, Cheryl Place, Gerald Regnaud, Christina Roy, Adrian Thibault, Bruce Weston and Brian Zeno.

Starksboro's own Professor Light-finger (Art Fulcher) delighted children and adults with his mystifying collection of magical medicines for mysterious maladies.

The Bandwagon schedule was temporarily interrupted by one of those grand crises that becomes an event all its own – a thunderstorm – sending the audience and performers into the refuge of Robinson School, a character-building experience on a humid, steamy night. Undaunted however, the schedule proceeded, carried onward by the musical talent and stamina of "The Highwaymen" a band from Burlington which includes Starksboro resident Rick Peyser.

The band settled into a classroom and played to a Standing-Room-Only audience, setting the school pulsating to rhythm, in tandem with the storm outside thundering a rhythm of its own.

While rain soaked the Bandwagon grounds, the situation within the school was cheek-to-jowl. Obviously a rescue was in order. Said rescue was promptly effected by the Starksboro Volunteer Fire Department under the direction of Fire Chief Fenwick Estey, who dispatched his men to make ready the Town Hall. They cleared aside the exhibit, "Starksboro Then and Now" and transported all the necessary accouterments for the remainder of the evening's events to the Hall.

Elsa Gilbertson, a 1976 graduate of Mount Abraham Union High School, delivered a "Bicentennial Minute", written by herself, which chronicled the struggles involved in Vermont's initial attempt to become the 14th state of the Union.

Elsa's reading was a fitting prologue to the Calvary Baptist Choir's musical "I Love America". This program, a cantata in celebration of our nation's ideals, was delivered with spirit and vigor. Individual selections were sung by Lessie Dunham, Lee Flint, Gareth Tobin and Director Sue-Carol Shepardson. Particularly notable was "Johnny Bull" sung by 9 year old Chip Flint. Gareth Tobin, a native of Starksboro, is the pastor of the Calvary Baptist Church of Essex Junction and sings with the choir.

A group from the Hinesburg Huff 'N Puffers, including Norman and Diane Cota of Starksboro, demonstrated the traditional Square Dance form. The winning ticket for the Meeting House Quilt Raffle was drawn — and won by a lady in New York State.

A this point, the rainstorm over, "The Highwaymen" moved to the Bandwagon Stage and resumed their music for an enthusiastic group of dancers, while the other scheduled events continued on stage in the Town Hall.

An original drama concluded the evening's live entertainment. "The Soft Soap Murder" written and directed by Rena Tobin and researched by Bertha Hanson, depicts the circumstances surrounding an authentic trial held in the 1830's at Asahel Wentworth's old tavern once located in back of Norma Wedge's house in the village of Starksboro. The cast consisted of Harold Gardner (Ezekiel Ross), Arthur Cota (Jessie Remington), Lee Wilson (First Justice Elijah Ferguson), Arthur Clifford (Second Justice, Samuel Bushnell), Joyce Wilson (Mary Brown), Janet Russell (Abigail Haskins), Norma Wedge (Annie Rounds), Harry Russell (Augustus White), Mark Whalon (Dr. Alfred Clark), and David Russell (Aaron Brown).

Refreshments of hot dogs, sandwiches, brownies, coffee and punch were served by the Meeting House Society throughout the afternoon and evening.

The Bandwagon, equipped with a selection of movies, brought the program to a close. Under the competent direction of Marcia Dominick, Bandwagon chairman, the day's events were an outstanding success.

The South Starksboro Homemakers sponsored a food sale and Bingo Party on Friday evening at the Jerusalem School. This provided an opportunity to visit the century old historic building, which was erected as a Free Will Baptist Church and a School House by the people of South Starksboro. The last teacher in this one-room school was Lucy Wyman who completed her work there in June 1968.

All of Starksboro came alive with a common interest, enthusiasm and anticipation as the entries for the Parade began to assemble on Saturday morning at Harvey's field just north of the Village. The excitement was contagious as a surrey from the Shelburne Museum and antique cars, rich with tradition, carried senior citizens, dressed in old time costumes, whose ancestors were early settlers of Starksboro. These residents are Mrs. Sewell Hallock (Grace), Mrs. Gale Mason (Ruth), Mrs. George Penrie (Nancy), Mrs. Newman Shepard (Mildred), Mrs. Harold Shivarette (Emma), Mrs. Floyd Smith (Martha), and Mrs. Amos Hanson (Ruth).

Three yoke of oxen owned by the Daniel Roberts Family of West Fairlee, brought a nostalgic feeling for the past when much of the farm work was done with oxen. Leroy Smith, who drove one yoke, is the son of the late Edgar Smith who owned one of the last ox-teams used in Starksboro.

Seven girls, four flag bearers and three baton twirlers, directed by Lexa Merrill, led the Parade. Christ the King Band from Burlington and the local band from Mt. Abraham Union High School provided music which added extra festivity. Marching were: the Robinson School children, dressed in Bicentennial costumes and each carrying an American flag: the Little League in their uniforms; clowns; "You've Come A Long Way Baby," a comic illustration; "Starksboro Then and Now" portrayed by Rachel McGovern and two of her friends. Several organizations entered floats. Among them were The Trailblazers 4-H Club, The First Baptist Church, Robinson School, the Snow Travelers, Miles Russell with a tractor and woodsplitter which was demonstrated by Harry Russell and Mack Moody, the South Starksboro Homemakers and the Purinton Farm. An added attraction was the 1976 Addison County Miss Agriculture and Dairy Princess. Members of two riding clubs and several local residents displayed their showmanship on horseback. Decorated bicycles gave a colorful note to the parade. Firetrucks from Starksboro, Bristol, Monkton and New Haven took part in the parade. The Bristol Rescue Squad participated and the ambulance remained on call throughout the day.

The parade ended at the Mike Mallow road, across from James Saunders' Homestead Acres Trailer Park. Judges Dickerman Orvis, Keith Hall and Robert Adsit, Jr. awarded ribbons for outstanding floats and other entries. Prize-winning floats were Starksboro Trailblazers 4-H Club – 1st, First Baptist Church – 2nd; Robinson School – 3rd. Awards for other entries were as follows: "You've Come A Long Way, Baby" – 1st, Surrey from Shelburne Museum – 2nd, Robinson School Indians – 3rd.

At the park, members of the Barbecue Committee had been busy preparing the chickens, potato salad, cole slaw, beans, rolls, cupcakes, punch and coffee which were served to 450 people. The delicious barbecue continued throughout the afternoon. A softball game was played between the Homestead A's and the Bristol A's. Little League, organized by Ralph Cota and George Elmore, and "Battle of the Sexes" games were also enjoyed by the fans. Participating in the "Battle of the Sexes" were Jane and Peg Estey, Janet Gendreau, Lexa Merrill, Ruth Elmore, Martha Cota, Peggy Zeno, Valerie Merrill, Vanessa Brace, Sandra Kelly, Nancy Pechie, Arthur Cota, Norman Cota, Melvin Kelly, Paul Zeno, Carroll Zeno, Jr., Joe Pechie, Jr., Brian Merrill, Maurice Horn, Ricky Mason and Peter Aube.

Saturday evening the Starksboro Snow Travelers held a Dance at the Town Hall. Music was furnished by Skip Little and the Country Folks from Charlotte.

A Hymn Sing and Informal Worship Service held in the South Starksboro Friends Meeting House at 4 o'clock Sunday afternoon, June 20, concluded the week's events. Richard Van Vliet of Lincoln played the fine, old pump organ. Bertha Hanson, after explaining the basic organization of the Society of Friends, gave a brief history of Quakers in Starksboro. A Meeting House was erected in the north part of town within the present limits of Green Mountain Cemetery in 1812 and stood there until 1859. South Starksboro Meeting House, built in 1826, is the last Quaker Meeting House in Vermont used exclusively by the Society of Friends. The half hour of silent worship which followed this presentation closed with the traditional Quaker custom of shaking hands with one's neighbor.

A collection of old pictures of South Starksboro was exhibited in the Meeting House hall. The Wedding Certificate signed at the marriage of William Hanson of Starksboro and Anna Grove of Bristol which took place in Lincoln Friends Meeting House in 1817, and the black Quaker bonnet later worn by Anna Grove Hanson as a Recorded Minister of the Starksborough Monthly Meeting of the Society of Friends, were also on display. A picnic, held indoors because of a sudden shower, provided opportunity for a delightful hour of conversation and fellowship.

Starksboro's Bicentennial Week recalled the Spirit of our Pioneers. Love of our town and our country was stimulated and expressed in many significant ways.

-Bicentennial Committee 1976

# 1780 *Starksboro* 1976

**1780**   On Nov. 9, *Starksboro was chartered by Vermont. Named in honor of General John Stark, one of the sixty-eight proprietors.*

**1787**   *John Ferguson from Nine Partners, NY, acquired land in Monkton, later included in Starksboro Village, where he and Thomas Vrandenburgh settled.*

**1788**   *In March settlement of Starksboro, as chartered, was begun by George Bidwell and Horace Kellogg from Hartford, CT. Bidwell located on the farm opposite Evelyn Nelson's house and Kellogg on the next place south.*

**1790**   *About this time David Kellogg, Oliver White, and Samuel Darrow settled in "Little Boston".*

**1796**   *Town organized. Warner Pierce elected Town Clerk.*

**1797**   *On March 4, 2,726 acres from the east side of Monkton was annexed to Starksboro by Act of Legislature.*

**1797**   *Samuel Hall purchased the place now owned by Muriel Brown. The house which was built for him is said to be the oldest frame dwelling in town.*

**1798**   *Methodist Episcopal Society was organized at the home of Abraham Bushnell. Elijah Hedding, who became Seventh Bishop of the Methodist Episcopal Church in America, later baptized in a nearby brook.*

**1799**   *David Hoag, Eligu Hoag and Stephen Carpenter erected the girst mill, now owned by Dr. Messer, at the Great Falls of Lewis Creek.*

**1799** About this time Richard Worth settled on the farm now owned by Ruth Mason. He drafted the first town plan and also brought from Monkton and planted the first apple tree in town.

**1800** About this time settlement of Hillsboro was begun by Samuel Hill. Brothers Lemuel, Thomas and Francis followed.

**1800** Joseph Sanborn, once a member of the Shaker Community in Canterbury, NH, settled on the Elizabeth Roberts place.

**1805** Samuel Bushnell opened a store on the site of the present Thibault Store.

**1806** James Kinsley located on the farm now owned by Arthur Clifford, the seventh generation of the family to occupy the place.

**1807** About this time Joshua Brown began settlement on Brown Hill.

**1812** Friends Meeting House built in present Green Mountain Cemetery. Sold and moved in winter of 1858-1859.

**1812** Jethro Stokes located on Mason Hill. Ebenezer Clifford, Deacon David Mason and Benjamin Ellison followed.

**1816** On June 27, Starksboro Post Office established.

**1821** On September 21, Free Will Baptist Society organized.

**1826** South Starksboro Friends Meeting House built. Remodeled 1871.

**1838** Methodist Meeting House built on present Arthur Clifford farm. Later sold and moved.

**1840** Village meeting House completed. Sanctuary used by Methodist, Baptist and Christian Societies. Basement was Town Hall.

**1850** About this time Irish immigrants came to "Little Ireland". Among them the Hannan, Casey, Conway, and Butler families.

**1857** On August 12, South Starksboro Post Office established. Discontinued April 30, 1902.

**1869** On December 15 the Free Will Baptist Meeting House, now the First Baptist Church, was dedicated.

**1874** South Starksboro Free Will Baptist Meeting was established. Met in Jerusalem School House until 1882 when discontinued.

**1898** Creamery established in Starksboro Village. Closed in 1974.

**1909** One-half mile wide strip of land from Monkton, lying mostly west of Route No. 116 between Floyd Shepard's house and the Hinesburg line, was annexed to Starksboro by Act of Legislature.

**1911** Starksboro Town Hall completed.

**1941** Robinson School, only two room school in town, opened.

**1973** Starksboro Municipal Building completed.

**1976** Starksboro Post Office Building erected by the town.

Bertha B. Hanson
Chairperson, Starksboro
Bicentennial Committee, 1976

# 1977

He was riding at a rapid pace over a bridge which had been thrown across a deep ravine. The plank broke, and both fore feet of the horse went through the opening. So sudden was the shock that the rider, Bishop Hedding, was thrown out of the sulky some eight or ten feet over the head of the horse, and for a time, lay insensible. The time: 1828. The place: Somewhere between Charlotte, Vermont and Chazy, New York. When the bishop regained consciousness, he found himself at the edge of a bridge, and right below him yawned a chasm twenty feet deep...His horse was caught, tangled in the harness. The good bishop paused, thanked God for being delivered, extricated the horse, and resumed his journey. He wrote his wife: "Through the mercy of God I am yet alive...Some people think it a wonderful privilege to be a Methodist Bishop; but if they had to drag around with me one year, I think they would change their opinion."

Thus begins the biography of Rev. Elijah Hedding, D.D., Seventh Bishop of the Methodist Episcopal Church in America, which appears in the booklet, "*Out of the North Country*", by Rev. Lewis N. Powell.

Elijah Hedding was born June 7, 1780, in Pine Plains, New York, the son of James and Ruth (Ferguson) Hedding. In 1791 the family moved to Starksboro, Vermont.

A few years later Abraham Bushnell and his wife, Mary, settled east of Starksboro Village on the place now owned by Mr. and Mrs. Ben Hirst. Mrs. Bushnell, a Methodist, persuaded Elijah, a wild youth known to be

***Elijah Hedding. D.D.*** *1780-1852*

an excellent reader, to read sermons to neighbors who gathered at her house on the Sabbath.

One evening after talking at length with Mrs. Bushnell, Elijah stopped in a grove on his way home and there committed his life to Christ. He said of that moment, "I laid my all – body, goods and all – for time and eternity upon the Altar, and have NEVER, never, taken them back."

Soon afterward he was baptized beside a brook near the Bushnell home. The stone upon which he knelt during the ceremony was subsequently engraved with the date. For many years it was to be seen in a near-by stone wall.

Almost as soon as he had been received into church membership, Elijah Hedding began what was to become his life work. In 1800, at the age of 19, he was given a preacher's license and set out to travel 300 miles on horseback each four weeks. On Sundays he held three meetings and on week days one or two meetings daily.

In 1803 at a conference in Cambridge, NY he was ordained by Bishop Whatcoat. Soon afterwards he began a thorough study of grammar. He also memorized the spelling and meaning of the words in three English dictionaries – Percy's, Walker's and Webster's.

For several years he worked in Vermont on the Barre Circuit and the Vershire Circuit. He also served the New England Conference in Connecticut, Massachusetts, New Hampshire and Maine.

The life of a circuit rider was often one of hardship. One cold winter night while traveling in Canada, Rev. Hedding shared the bed with a colleague. The next morning it was found that the colleague's feet had frozen while he slept.

In his journal Elijah Hedding wrote: "The woods are my study; the bible and the "elder" scripture my textbooks. I am glad during the summer to get into the woods and find an hour or two to read my Bible, and some other religious books I carry in my saddle bag. In the winter I am glad of the same privilege, by the fireside in a small log cabin of but one room, and the fire surrounded by a family of children."

"During the time I was single," wrote Bishop Hedding, "I traveled on the average of 3,000 miles a year...and preached nearly every day...all the pay I received in 10 years was $450...One year, I received on my circuit, exclusive of traveling expenses, three dollars and twenty-five cents. This was made up to $21 by the conference. My pantaloons were often patched upon the knees and the sisters often showed me their kindness by turning an old coat for me."

The young minister first met Lucy Blish, a young lady from Gilsom, CT, in Plattsburgh, NY in 1801. There were married in 1810.

In 1824 Elijah Hedding was elected Bishop of the Methodist Episcopal Church in America. His work covered a territory comprised of New England and New York, with frequent trips to Canada. He established the "Zion Herald", a Methodist publication, and made the plans for establishing the well known Cazenovia Seminary in Lansing, NY. He also compiled a hymnal for the use in his denomination.

Bishop Hedding died in Poughkeepsie, NY, April 9, 1852. Near the city a beautiful monument has been erected. The inscription reads in part: "He was, for fifty-one years, an itinerant minister, and for 28, a bishop in the Methodist Episcopal Church."

In his home church, the Starksboro Village Meeting House, one of the stained glass Memorial Windows commemorates his life and work. His portrait hangs in the upstairs entrance hall.

In her book, *"One Hundred Fifty Years of Methodism in Barre, Vermont"*, the late Constance Eastman Davis, wife of former Governor Deane Davis, paid tribute to Bishop Hedding: "He was a man of commanding presence and powerful voice, a born leader..." Methodism claims him as one of its truly great.

Bertha B. Hanson
1977 Town Report

# 1978

The earliest school record in Starksboro, dated March 1805, states: "The Scholars numbered and found to be one hundred and eighty-nine." By 1813 there were eight school districts in town. At the annual Town Meeting March 6, 1832 the town was divided into seventeen school districts. Over the years these districts have merged. The last merger was 1968 when Jerusalem School in South Starksboro was merged into Robinson School in Starksboro Village.

The first school building in Starksboro Village, known as the "Center School House", stood on the spot where Greta Knox's house is now located. It served Starksboro Village and the area within walking distance until the latter part of the nineteenth century when the townspeople began to feel that a new, larger and more impressive building should be constructed in the "First District".

On April 27, 1892 the town acquired a deed from Page Smith to a half acre of land adjoining the Baptist Parsonage Lot. There a one room school house topped with a cupola was constructed.

In 1941 the Village School was remodeled and enlarged to accommodate pupils from both the Village District and the North School District. There were two classrooms on the upper level and school lunch facilities on the lower level. The new building was named "Robinson School" in honor of Albert J. Robinson, the owner of Mountain View Creamery, who provided the necessary funds to complete the project.

By the fall of 1953 the consolidation of districts and increased school population made it necessary to utilize the north room on the lower level as a classroom for first and second grades.

The playground was enlarged in 1964 by the purchase of additional land from Mr. and Mrs. Harold Shivarette.

In the fall of 1968 Mt. Abraham Union High School opened with accommodations for grades 7 through 12. Elementary pupils from Jerusalem School in South Starksboro were then transported to the Village School.

The elementary school population continued to grow rapidly. A citizens study committee organized in the fall of 1972, reported to the School Board in January 1973, suggesting various alternatives for accommodating the increased number of students. The School Board decided to convert the south room on the lower level, previously used as a kitchen-cafeteria, to a classroom which was ready for use in the Fall of 1973. School lunches were served in the Town Hall.

In January, 1976, a second citizens study committee recommended the construction of a two room addition with a basement which could eventually be converted into two additional classrooms. An architect was engaged to prepare preliminary plans for the proposed wing. By this time overcrowding at Robinson School had become an emergency situation, adversely affecting both learning opportunities for children and the efforts of the teaching staff in the performance of their duties.

Early in the fall of 1976 the Board of Selectmen and the Board of School Directors learned that federal funds for municipal construction projects might be available under the Local Public Works Capital Development and Investment Act of 1976. A public hearing was held at the Town Hall on October 8 to discuss the proposed addition and an application for federal funds. A model of the proposed wing, together with the architects' drawings, was presented for the consideration of the townspeople. An informal ballot indicated that the voters were in favor of the new addition and also in favor of making an application for federal funds.

At a Special Town and Town School District Meeting, held November 22, 1976, the voters approved the filing of an application under the Local Public Works Capital Development and Investment Act of 1976 for federal funds to be used for the construction of an addition to the Robinson School House. Ruford Brace, Selectman, was appointed official Representative for the town. The application, submitted November 30, was accepted but not funded due to insufficient funds.

*The Village School, 1892/1941.* **(A22)**

*Robinson School.*

***John Dike's Sawmill*** *located across from the current Robinson School Parking Lot.*

On February 28, 1977 town officials learned that there might be another opportunity to apply for federal funds under the 1977 Amendment to the Local Public Works Capital Development and Investment Act of 1976. An application was submitted on August 10. On September 16 the town was mailed an Offer of Grant in the amount of $169,000.00 This was accepted on September 20.

In the meantime, in order to accommodate the increased number of students enrolled at Robinson School, the School Board purchased a mobile classroom from the Thetford School District. This was installed in August 1977.

Bids for the construction of the new wing were opened on November 23. The contract was awarded to Quality Construction Company, Richmond, Vermont, Louis G. Roy, Owner. On-site labor began January 3, 1978. However, due to extreme weather conditions, work was discontinued until April.

Equipment for the classrooms in the new addition was purchased with $4,500.00 of the L.P.W. grant money.

School opened September 18, 1978 with 135 students in attendance. The new wing contained four classrooms – two on the lower level and two on the upper level. The mobile classroom accommodated first grade students. The north upper level room in the old building continued to be used as a classroom while the south room was partitioned to provide a principal's office, teachers' room, and remedial reading room. The spacious hall furnished room for the school library. The south room on the lower level, formerly the kitchen-cafeteria, became the kitchen. A newly installed commercial dishwasher insured maximum sanitation for cooking and eating utensils. The north room on the lower level was remodeled as a dining room.

An open house to celebrate the completion of the new addition was held Thursday evening, November 30, 1978. The new wing was dedicated to Ruby B. Craig. Arthur Clifford, Town and Town School District Moderator, presented Mrs. Craig with two plaques, one for herself and another to be hung in the hall of the new addition. The inscription reads: "As an expression of gratitude for her assistance, guidance, and long hours of unceasing effort which resulted in the building of these classrooms, we, the people of Starksboro, hereby dedicate this addition to Ruby B. Craig."

Bertha B. Hanson
Town Report 1978

# 1979

HISTORIC ELM
PLANTED IN THE 1800's, THIS TREE
IS HEREBY DESIGNATED A HISTORIC
LANDMARK TO BE HONORED AND
PRE-SERVED FOR FUTURE GENERATIONS
ELM RESEARCH INSTITUTE
HARRISVILLE, N.H. 03450

TOWN OF
## Starksboro, Vermont

Elm Tree on Gilbertson Lawn
Starksboro — Monkton Line
To 1797

## Annual Report
### 1978-1979

T his inscription appears on the plaque which Elsa Gilbertson received in 1974 for the large elm tree on the Gilbertson lawn. Located 16 feet east of highway No. 116, it stands on the old charter line of the town of Monkton. When a 2,726 acre tract from Monkton was annexed to Starksboro by Act of Legislature in 1797 the southern section of the Monkton-Starksboro line was moved one mile to the westward. This old elm is one of the few remaining landmarks identifying the original town line.

The Gilbertson property is part of the "Old John Dike Farm" north of Starksboro Village. First settled in 1797 by David and Sara Meader, Quakers from New Hampshire, it became the property of Jarvis and Susannah Hoag in 1835. Along with other agricultural pursuits, they operated a fruit tree nursery there until 1855 when they sold the place to John and Susan Layn. The Layns transferred the property to their daughter and son-in-law, Jane and Henry Dike, in 1870. It descended in turn to their son, John, and his wife, Mabel, who sold it in 1943. Thereafter it changed hands several times before George and Magnhild Gilbertson of Greenwich, Connecticut bought the buildings and land immediately surrounding them in 1963.

George Gilbertson was a retired United States Naval Officer. Magnhild is native of Norway. Together they operated a small corporation known as AEGIR, a business which Magnhild continued for several years after her husband's death. She also served as Town Clerk in Starksboro in 1973.

With the passing years the stately old elm became a daily source of enjoyment to the Gilbertson family – Magnhild, Elsa and Lars. As they watched it in the changing season they began to feel that this majestic tree should have a name. They chose to call it "Yggdrasill". The name comes from Norse mythology. According to legend the universe is supported by a great tree, Yggdrasill, "House of Yggr, the Terrible One." The roots of the tree grow through the world of the living and the dead. It is watered by a sacred well at the foot of the tree. There Uror, Destiny, decides the fates of men. "Life-giving dew falls on the earth from its branches and a goat that pastures on its leaves gives mead for the gods to drink. The tree also suffers: a winged dragon gnaws at its roots; in the branches an eagle sits and a squirrel runs up and down the tree stirring up strife between the eagle and the dragon."

At a height of 5 feet from the ground Yggdrasill has a circumference of 14 feet 8 inches. This indicates that the elm was prob-

*The Dike Place, c.1810/ c.1880. Henry and Jane Dike lived here for many years and added the second story to the house. Their son, John, and grandson, Henry, also lived here. The place is now the home of Magnhild Gilbertson.* **(12)**

ably planted about 1800. "No other tree is comparable to this unique American species," states the Elm Institute in their letter to Elsa.

Yggdrasill became the victim of Dutch Elm Disease in 1978. This historic elm still stands, however, "an awesome spirit of beauty and might," as Elsa and Lars described it in its prime.

Bertha B. Hanson
1979  Town Report

Starksboro was chartered November 9, 1780 by Thomas Chittenden, Governor of Vermont, to David Bridia and sixty-seven others, among them General John Stark for whom the town was named.

The Starksboro Town Bicentennial Celebration was held at the Town Hall on December 5, 1980. It was well attended. Delicious food was provided by townspeople and visiting friends.

The evening program began with music by Fay and Dudley Leavitt of Lincoln. Especially outstanding was their presentation of "The Ballad of Freeman James", a song which they have written about a Starksboro lad who served as a drummer boy throughout the Civil War. His drum is now in Sheldon Museum in Middlebury.

A slide presentation "Starksboro Then and Now", with narrative by Bertha Hanson followed. Pictures of old houses and a few new ones, stores, mills, public buildings, people and events pertinent to the history of the Town were included.

"The Soft Soap Murder", a play written by Rena Tobin, depicted an exciting event in Starksboro's early history. The Actors, all local people, were Harold Gardner, David Russell, William Coon, Arthur Clifford, Rev. Robert Martens, Fenwick Estey, Arthur Cota, Norma Wedge, Marilyn Martens and Denise Vantine.

"Starksboro Events, National Bicentennial 1976", presented by Paulita Estey, featured slides of the week-long celebration held in town at that time.

The program closed with musical selections by the Leavitts.

-1980 Starksboro Bicentennial
  Committee

On March 5, 1774 James Kinsley of Kelsa on the River Tweed in Scotland, then a young man sixteen years of age, boarded a ship bound for the new world. Arriving in the colonies after seven weeks spent crossing the Atlantic he soon became established in Maine. It was from there that he enlisted in the Revolutionary War.

James married Mary Call as his first wife. For a time the family lived in Springfield, Vermont. Attracted by unsettled land, James, his second wife Buradell Cheney, together with James, Jr., a son of his first marriage, and possible other family members, moved to Starksboro arriving, according to tradition, in 1806. There they selected a home site. On December 19, 1807, James Sr., paid $450 to Charles Calkins of Hinesburg for lot no. 701 to the right of James Evarts containing approximately 100 acres. This lot, where the Kinsley's had doubtless already begun settlement, is a part of the farm now owned by Arthur Clifford, a seventh generation descendant, and operated by Arthur and his son, Eric, a member of the eighth generation. It lies about 200 rods east of Route 116. There, in what is now a large meadow east of the Carroll Hill-Harry Russell sugar works, James Sr. and James Jr.

built a log cabin. Only a few years ago a log from this cabin could still be seen in that field.

James Sr. died April 23, 1813. James Jr., anxious to keep the farm he had helped his father wrest from the wilderness, bought the shares of the estate set to his sister and brothers. In 1818 he purchased a part of Lot 721 thereby extending his holdings to the "old line road", now Route No. 116, which had already been laid out approximately on the original Starksboro-Monkton line. Other land was soon added, some of which was across the road in what was then the town of Monkton.

James Jr. married Betsey Pearsons. Members of the Methodist Episcopal Society, they felt strongly that a meeting house was a necessity to a growing and prosperous neighborhood. James Jr. became a leading member of the Starksboro North Meeting House Building Committee. His name, with a subscription of $100, headed the list of twenty-eight Starksboro, Monkton, and Hinesburg men who sponsored the project. On January 9, 1839, in consideration of $12.50, James deeded a tract of land "...on which stands a building now occupied for a religious meeting house ..." to the Methodist Episcopal Society of Starksboro,

92

*Home Farm of Arthur & Esther Clifford.* **(49)**

Monkton and Hinesburg. This meeting house stood between Arthur Clifford's present tenement house and the house owned by Mrs. Cora Billado. Years later, moved to a new location north of the house now occupied by Mrs. Billado, it became a horse barn. It has since been demolished.

After the death of James Junior's first wife he married in 1843 Sally (Pierce) Kinsley, widow of Milo William Kinsley, and soon purchased the Starksboro Village farm now known as the Leroy Smith Place (Lewis Creek Farm). A stained glass window in the Starksboro Village Meeting House dedicated to James and Sally Kinsley bears witness to their continued effort in behalf of the Methodist Episcopal Society.

Charles L. Kinsley, son of James Jr. and Betsey, became the owner of the old farm in the north part of town. His wife was Hester Caswell whose family were early settlers of Huntington. Under the management of Charles and Hester the farm continued to improve and expand. It is not known just when or by whom the house now occupied by Arthur Clifford was built but that Charles and Hester lived there is an established fact. They had three daughters, each of whom had a part in the Kinsley property. Betsey married Israel Eddy. They built the house now owned by Cora Billado. Emerette married Madison Tyler and they lived in the former Chester Bidwell Place, now the home of Carroll Hill and Harry Russell. Harriet married Wallace N. Hill and stayed in her old home. Wallace was prominent in town affairs, serving as Town Representative and Addison County Senator.

In 1896, Nina, daughter of Wallace and Harriett (Kinsley) Hill, married Arthur Clifford. Arthur and Nina remained on the old Kinsley-Hill place where they carried on a very successful farming operation. Their only child, Harold Clifford, inherited the property. In 1921 he married Martha Eddy. It was on this farm that their children, Arthur and Earlene (Clifford) Gardner grew up. Harold and Martha lived there until the marriage of their son, Arthur, to Esther Merrill in 1950. They then moved to Starksboro Village. Arthur and Esther took over the farm. Under Arthur's management the farm expanded to include the so-called Fred Brown place where the house now occupied by Eric Clifford is located and a part of the old John Brooks property, a portion of which became the site of the new house where Martha Clifford and Harold and Earlene Gardner now live. Arthur built the first free stall barn and installed the first milking parlor in this area in 1959.

After graduating from UVM, Eric, only son of Arthur and Esther, joined his father on the farm. Arthur and Esther, together with Eric and his wife, the former Jane Magnus, now operate the place as a family farm. It

*Home of Cora Billado, c.1875. Ernest and Madge Eddy lived here before they moved to the village.* **(50)**

*Home of Arthur and Esther Clifford, c.1840.* **(49)**

continues to be a successful business enterprise which keeps pace with the new agricultural development.

The Kinsley-Hill-Clifford Place has the unique distinction of being the only farm in Starksboro which has been passed down in an unbroken line from generation to generation of the family who first cleared and settled the land.

Bertha B. Hanson
1981  Town Report

***The Clifford Farm*** *after Route 116 was paved.*

***Frank Smith Family House, c.1870.*** *Now the home of Eric and Jane Clifford.* **(9)**

**Brooks Place, c.1900.** *Stood on the site of Harold Clifford's present dwelling. House burned in the 1920's when Chase Stokes owned it. Part of Monkton until 1909. Anson and Sylvia Brown (Bertha's parents) on lawn. Earlene Clifford lives on this site today.*

# 1982

Starksboro, chartered by the State of Vermont in 1780, was first settled in 1788. The town was organized in March 1796 at a Town Meeting held in the log cabin home of one of the early settlers. Since the minutes of the meeting have been lost we know very little about what took place at that time.

Town Meeting Records began in 1808 with a meeting held at the School House in the South School District. From that time until 1839 Town Meetings were usually held at the Center School in the First School District. The Center School was a one room building located in Starksboro Village on the present site of the Greta Knox residence (next door to Rublee's Farm). Occasionally, however, a meeting was scheduled in Samuel Bushnell's store, Elijah Ferguson's dwelling, or at Wentworth's Inn.

With the passing years church membership and the wealth of the townspeople increased to the point that in 1838 the Methodists, Free Will Baptists, and members of the Christian Church felt it feasible to undertake the building of a meeting house in Starksboro Village. At the Annual March Meeting in 1838 the Town subscribed "$400 to be paid to the building committee of the

contemplated meeting house on the first day of October next" to defray the expense of building a "Town Room". This room, located in the basement of the new building, was accessible only from the outside. Though the Meeting House was not completed until 1840, a Special Meeting was held in the new Town Room on "Monday the 2nd day of December 1839."

Early in the twentieth century the need for more space, not only for Town Meeting, but also for other community activities became apparent. A committee was appointed at Town Meeting in 1909 to see about the possibility of purchasing the Village Meeting House for a Town Hall. It consisted of the three Selectmen, namely C. F. Clifford, J. W. Casey, and E.S. Follansbee, together with W. N. Hill. At a Special Meeting held on October 28, 1909, it was decided to "leave the matter of the Town Hall" to the committee. Upon their recommendation the Town voted on March 1, 1910 to appropriate a sum of money not to exceed $4,000 to buy a building lot and erect a Town Hall. The building committee was to consist of the Selectmen, W.N. Hill and Edmond Hannon.

On March 10, 1910 Betsey J. Eddy, in consideration of $150.00, deeded to the

***Town Hall, 1911.*** *By the early 1900s the town had outgrown its meeting space in the basement of the Village Meeting House. The Town Hall was built and furnished for a total cost of $4,096.15 in 1911. This commodious building was the center of community pride and numerous activities, such as town meetings, plays, traveling shows, dances, and suppers, were held here until the 1984 addition of the elementary school was built. It is simply detailed except for the front porch with turned posts and the paneled double doors. Inside is beaded board wainscoting and a stage with a rare painted curtain.* **(A27)**

***Benjamin L. Knight House, c.1850.*** *This may be two houses that were joined together. Dr. Friend Hall lived on this site in the early 1800s. The house is best known as the home of Benjamin L. Knight, who operated a carding mill below the Hoag Grist Mill on the great falls of the Lewis Creek (on State's Prison Hollow Road) and originally lived in the house still there. This house is Greek Revival, with pilasters around the doors*

*and on the corners, and peaked lintels over the windows. It also has a very old barn in the rear. Knight was noted for his business sense, but he was one of the men who founded the Starksboro Copper Mining Company, chartered in 1866, to look for minerals on Brown Hill. Located on the North side of the Town Hall, it is now the home of Donald Shepard.* **(A28)**

Town of Starksboro a rectangular plot of land with a 45-foot frontage and a 91-foot depth. The Town Hall was constructed that year. Charles Miller was paid $3,450.00 for labor and material. L.G. and F.S. Ferguson received $90.00 for the kerosene lights and fixtures. Curtains and fixtures cost $37.05, a fire hydrant and pipe $37.60. G. W. Clifford received $2.00 for work on the ditch. Readsboro Chair Manufacturing Company was paid $281.50 for the folding chairs which are still being used. The total cost of the land, building and furnishings, as recorded in the Auditor's Report for 1911, was $4,096.15.

The Town Hall, a two-story rectangular structure with gable end fronting on the highway and a small porch covering the entry way, occupied most of the lot. No provision was made for hitching horses. It was not thought necessary. Both the Baptist Church and the Village Meeting House had horse sheds. People who did not own a stall in one of these structures brought hitching weights and left their horses and wagons beside the street. Since cars were few there was no traffic problem.

The new Town Hall became a center for community activity. The Town placed a safe for the town records in the lower room. A small room on the right of the entrance hall contained shelves for such records as did not need the protection of a vault. Town Meetings were held in the lower room until 1949. General Election voting took place upstairs. During the Christmas season the Christian Culture Club used the stage upstairs to present their annual play. Their sale was held downstairs and a supper was served there. For many years this was one of the most important social events in town. Traveling companies presented plays at various times. Local groups held dances there. In the 1920's the Town Schools began holding eighth grade graduation exercises in the upper room.

In 1930, when electricity became available in Starksboro, Hervey Hanson wired the Town Hall at a cost of $266.33. The first light bill received from Green Mountain Power Corporation was for 57 cents.

In 1950 Town Meeting was moved upstairs because the space downstairs had become too small to accommodate the voters. This arrangement continued until 1980 when it became evident that it was unfair for the handicapped to have to contend with stairs at Town Meeting and Election. Therefore Town Meeting, beginning in 1981, and all elections thereafter were scheduled to be held in the lower room. That year a ramp was built to insure handicapped access to the Town Hall.

Two major problems still remain to be solved however. There is insufficient parking space near the Town Hall where no additional land is available for purchase. Moreover space is becoming inadequate, both upstairs and down, for the voters at Town Meeting and for the townspeople at

*Starksboro Village Street Scene c.1900.*
*Parsonage and Barn. Note narrow front porch.*
*Oletha Bickford Apartment House.*
*Lyle & Joyce Shepard's Home. Note ginger bread trim*
*Village Meeting House behind the tree.*
*Greta Knox house.*
*Leslie Rublee's home. Photo courtesy of Ruth Hanson.*

special events which attract large audiences.

In the fall of 1981 a study committee was appointed to look into the needs of the town, one of the most rapidly growing communities in the state, and for additional school space. One of the options which is presently being explored is the possibility of moving the Town Hall to land to be acquired for the purpose of enlarging the existing school facility and playground. If this should prove feasible for the Town Hall, one of the town's historic buildings might thus be preserved as a useful part of the town's heritage.

Bertha Hanson
1982 Town Report

*She added the following note: The Town Hall was not moved. It stands on the original lot.*

# 1983

Arthur Eddy Clifford was born August 29, 1923, the son of Harold W. and Martha (Eddy) Clifford. A descendant of James Kinsley, a native of Scotland, who purchased land in Starksboro in 1807, Arthur is the seventh generation of the family to own and operate the farm where he now resides.

His first eight years of schooling were received at the one room North School in Starksboro. He then enrolled in Hinesburg High School where he graduated with honors in 1942. After attending the University of Vermont for a year he returned to the home farm. During his student year and afterward as a young farmer, he was active in Future Farmers of America. At the convention of the National Future Farmers of America, held in Kansas City in 1944 he was elected Vice President of the National organization.

In 1950 Arthur married Esther Merrill and together they took over the management of the farm. Their children, Eric and Mary, grew up there. Over the years the farm has been expanded to include the so-called Fred Brown Place where the house now occupied by their son and daughter-in-law, Eric and Jane, is located and also a part of the John Brooks farm, a portion of which became the site of the new home occupied by Arthur's mother, Martha, and his brother-in-law and sister, Harold and Earlene Gardner. In 1959 Arthur built the first free stall barn and installed the first milking parlor in this area. He was honored in 1968 as Vermont Dairyman of the year. The hundred head Holstein dairy farm is now operated by Arthur in partnership with his son, Eric, whose small daughter, Elizabeth, represents the ninth generation of the family to live on the farm.

Arthur bought the so-called Pete Haskins Place on the hill east of Starksboro Village in 1969. Soon afterward he built a four acre trout pond in the mucky area long known as "Black Ash Swamp". Arthur's daughter, Mary, dubbed the place "Muck Hill", thus it came about that the road leading to the pond is now known as Muck Hill Road. The pond, now flanked by a small water fall, a canoe landing and a pier is enjoyed as a recreation spot by the family, their friends, and neighbors. The property has now been expanded into a 600-acre tree farm. About nine miles of logging roads have been constructed up the steep hillsides to enable easy access to wood and timber. The tree farm project has proved so successful that the State Environmental Conservation Agency honored Arthur as the 1982 Vermont Outstanding Tree Farmer.

For many years Arthur has been active in the Green Mount Cemetery Association in Starksboro. He has served as a member of the Board of Directors and also as manager of the cemetery since 1957.

Since 1948 Arthur has held several town offices. He has served as Auditor, Selectman, First Grand Juror and Moderator at various times. In 1983 he announced that he was retiring as Moderator after serving two stints in office, six years between 1952 and 1958 and twelve years between 1971 and 1983, making a total of eighteen years in that office – the longest total number of years anyone has ever served the town in that capacity. At Town Meeting on March 1, 1983 Selectman William Coon, on behalf of the townspeople, presented him with a plaque in appreciation for his outstanding and dedicated service to the town. Acknowledging the gift Arthur said: "It has been a pleasure to serve all these years."

By unanimous and resounding voice vote the townspeople voted to dedicate this year's Town Report to Arthur Clifford.

Bertha B. Hanson
1983  Town Report

*Arthur E. Clifford*

## Starksboro Volunteer Fire Department

On May 20, 1959 seventeen Starksboro men, namely, Ruford Brace, Richard Burbank, Roy Carlson, Denis Corriveau, Arthur Cota, Fenwick Estey, Wayne Hill, Frederic McGovern, Robert M. Merrill, Antoine Parker, Leslie Rublee, Leroy Smith, Lloyd Stearns, Frank Strong, Russell Tatro, Charles Thibault, and Frederick Wedge, met in the basement of the Starkboro Village Meeting House (then known as the Starksboro Community House) to discuss organizing a volunteer fire department for the Town of Starksboro. Four men from the North Ferrisburg Volunteer Fire Department assisted in organizing the new department which was officially named "Starksboro Volunteer Fire Department." It was decided to keep the organization completely separate from town government. Officers elected were: President and Fire Chief – Leroy Smith; Assistant Fire Chief – Frank Strong; Secretary- Fenwick Estey; Treasurer – Howard Stearns. After a vote of thanks to the ladies who served lunch a collection was taken "to pay for the doughnuts and to start finances in the treasury." The first donation

*Volunteer Fire Department* – *original five members remaining* – *(left to right) Fenwick Estey, Charlie Thibault, Arthur Cota, Leroy Smith & Leslie Rublee.*

of $50.00 was made to the fire department by Harry Strong.

At a special meeting held May 29 of that year five members were elected to serve as trustees: Chief Leroy Smith, Lloyd Stearns, Roy Carlson, Fenwick Estey and Frank Strong. It was voted to incorporate the department and adopt the recommended by-laws. It was also decided to sponsor a turkey dinner on June 28, the last Sunday in June. This has since been the established date for the Fireman's Annual Turkey dinner.

By November 16 of that year the Fire Department was prosperous enough to order a Darley portable pump on trial. It arrived January 21 and was soon after tried out in States Prison Hollow. Since it performed well it was purchased for $172.43. This pump is still in use on the tank truck.

The first Fire School, held in cooperation with the Huntington Fire Department, was held at Robinson School in 1960. It was a 45-hour Basic Firemanship Course sponsored by the Vermont Firefighters Association in collaboration with the Vermont Department of Education. The course began on April 4 and was completed on June 21. Each fireman who completed the full course was awarded a certificate from the State Firefighters Association by Clayton Welch, the instructor in charge. He remarked that "they were the best group of men he had ever taught."

In June 1960 a Ford Platform Truck was acquired through Civil Defense. In September two fuel tanks were installed on the truck at Robert M. Merrill's Garage. The vehicle was then driven to Baldwin Pond where the tanks were filled with water. A 136-foot extension ladder and a 14-foot roof ladder were soon purchased and added to the truck. The newly purchased vehicle was housed in the old town garage located on the east side of highway No. 116 directly across from Robinson School.

That year marked the beginning of the Annual Ladies Night sponsored in appreciation of the help which firemen's wives had given with fund raising events. It was held at the Lincoln Inn December 6, 1960, with 14 firemen and their guests in attendance.

The big fund-raising event of 1960 was an auction held in Arthur Cota's new barn on October 8. The Department realized $633.80 from it.

The biggest fires attended between 1960 and 1966 while the Department was using its first fire truck were: Roy Bartlett's Camp, Lloyd Tatro's house, Clifford Hanson's barn in Monkton, William Jameson's house in States Prison Hollow, Ernest Quitner's two-car garage, Robert Adsit, Senior's Camp and the Doland House in Starksboro Village then owned by Gilbert Farnham.

The Department was accepted as a member of the Addison County Firefighters Association on June 18, 1961. A contract for mutual aid for the Town of Starksboro in conjunction with all Fire Departments in Addison County was signed by the Trustees and the Town Selectmen on February 15 of that year.

Two more outstanding events occurred in 1961. On February 21 eight complete outfits consisting of helmets, coats and boots were ordered. A surplus Darley front-mounted pump was ordered for the Ford Truck on May 15.

The by-laws were amended on April 24, 1962. The monthly meeting date was changed from the third Monday to the first Monday of each month.

The tragic death of Assistant Chief Frank Strong on June 25, 1963 saddened every member of the department. Frank, the only man who died while an active fireman, was an enthusiastic, hard-working member of the department who cheerfully performed any and every duty asked of him. It was on August 5 of that year that Fenwick Estey told the Department that his sister, Mrs. Frank Strong, wished to give the building known as the "Walston Store" for use as a Fire Station in memory of Frank. The department and the townspeople are proud of The Fire Station. They greatly appreciate this generous gift.

In May 1966 the firemen were pleased to be able to purchase a 1950 Seagraves Truck which was at that time, the latest model fire truck in the county. To finance the purchase the trustees borrowed $2,000.00 from the First National Bank of Bristol, signing the note themselves. The old Ford truck continued in use as a tank truck.

July 1967 saw the installation of eight Red Phones to receive fire calls. No longer did the person receiving the first call have to contact each and every fireman on several party lines with only the assistance of the fire siren on Leroy Smith's barn.

Ladies night was held at the Old Lantern in Charlotte for the first time on October 16, 1968. There an orchestra and dancing could be enjoyed. This has since been the established place for this annual event.

When, on May 3, 1971, Leroy Smith declined to serve as Fire Chief any longer, Frederic Wedge was elected to fill that office.

An Army surplus 6 x 6 truck was acquired from the Department of Forest and Parks at no cost in June, 1972. It was painted and the old red portable tank was mounted on the truck by the Middlesex Fire Equipment Company for $1,107.50.

The following year the department received $800.00 from the IBM Community Support Program.

Fenwick Estey became Fire Chief in May 1974. He has served in that capacity ever since.

In March 1974 radios were purchased for the firemen. The base was installed in the home of Chief Fenwick Estey where it has since remained.

An outstanding event in the history of Starksboro was the 1976 Bicentennial Celebration held June 13 through 20. The weeklong celebration opened with a Worship Service at the First Baptist Church. The firemen attended in body. After the service they officiated at the flag raising ceremony on the church lawn when the American flag and the bicentennial flag were officially raised to fly over the town during the week's festivities. At 12 noon the annual Fire Department Turkey Dinner was served in the Town Hall. On June 22 the firemen with the Starksboro fire trucks took part in the well-organized parade which wound its way from Harvey's meadow north of the village to the Mike Mallow Road opposite Jim Saunders' trailer park south of town where it disbanded.

On February 7, 1977 the Department voted to purchase a 1959 pumper from Danbury, Conn. at a cost of $5,000.00.

In November 1978 it was decided to ask

the voters of the town to allow the Department to construct an addition to the Jerusalem Schoolhouse to be used as a substation. At the Annual Town Meeting in March 1979 the town voted to approve the addition. The addition, known as Station No. 2, was built that summer. The 1959 pumper is now housed there.

On June 8, 1978 Mrs. Harry Strong gave land adjacent to Fire House No. 1 for future expansion of the fire station.

A chicken barbecue was held at Station No. 2 in the summer of 1980. This has become an annual fund-raising event. Held on the last Sunday of July it features fun and games for young and old.

In recent years several improvements and acquisitions have been made. A 1959 American LaFrance 750 pumper was purchased in 1979. In the fall of 1981 the tanker was repowered by a 28 motor and five speed transmission. The motor in the American LaFrance was rebuilt in the summer of 1982. During the winter of 1983 a new tank was constructed for the tanker and the truck was painted.

The department now has a membership of 25 firemen and five junior firemen.

On May 18 and 20, 1984 the Starksboro Volunteer Fire Department celebrated its twenty-fifth anniversary. The celebration began with a potluck supper held Saturday

*Left to right:* Percy Jennings, Norman Cota, Josh Martell, Nate Goldman, Tim Porter, Fenwick Estey, Tony Porter, Tom Estey, Leslie Rublee, Roger Thibault, Dave Orvis, Matt Estey, Lawrence Martell. **Kneeling:** Eric Cota, Bobby Briggs.
**Not Pictured:** Dave Bedard, Dennis Casey, Arthur Cota, Mike Gilley, Pat Hendee, Hugh Johnson, Bill Lafountain, Leroy Smith, Adie Thibault, Charles Thibault.

evening, May 19, in the Town Hall. Five of the men present who helped organize the department in 1959 are still active at the present time; namely Leroy Smith, Fenwick Estey, Arthur Cota, Leslie Rublee and Charles Thibault. Highlights of the evening were the reading by Rena Tobin of an original poem entitled "Our Volunteer Firemen," the presentation to the Department of a plaque by the Selectmen and the presentation to individual firemen of awards and certificates. The guest speaker, Ray Davison, had worked with the department for many years as Vermont State Firefighter instructor. The program also included comments by Roger Stone, County representative to the State and Roger Young, Vice President of the Addison County Firefighters Association.

The Open House, held on Sunday, May 20 from 12 noon to 5 p.m. at the Fire House, featured demos throughout the day, free gifts for kids, and refreshments. Tot finders, phone stickers and informational brochures were also available. Among items for sale were smoke alarms, painters caps and T-shirts.

The Starksboro Volunteer Fire Department thus concluded twenty-five years of faithful and outstanding service to the Town of Starksboro.

Research - Ila Smith
Narrative - Bertha B. Hanson
1983-1984

## The Municipal Building -
## Post Office Complex

The Town Municipal building was constructed in 1973 with Revenue Sharing funds. At that time large boulders already on the property were pushed into place to form a retaining wall in front of the building. The wall held the bank in place but added little to the landscape.

One of the oldest organizations in town is the Friendship Homemaker's Club. Homemaker's Clubs were organized through the Vermont Extension Service as a result of the Smith-Lever Bill passed by Congress in 1914 for "the purpose of diffusing...useful and practical information on subjects relating to agriculture and home economics." The Starksboro Club, probably organized about 1920, has sponsored many community and school related projects. Each year the members make and sell a quilt to raise funds for projects the club wishes to subsidize. The group often discussed the need to improve the landscaping around the municipal building. They decided to offer a donation of $500.00 toward the cost of constructing a new retaining wall. At town meeting in March, 1985 the voters agreed to

match this with a sum of money not to exceed $1,000.00.

Early that summer David Mason, a local stone mason who is well known for his outstanding ability to design and build unique and beautiful stone walls, was hired for the job. Using stone from the old wall and others, many of which were donated by interested local residents for a special spot, David constructed a new wall with a walk and steps leading to the front door of the municipal building. An inviting stone bench, placed near the town war memorial, completed his work. The total cost to the town of tearing out the old wall, completing the cost of constructing the new one, and landscaping the grounds was $831.14.

Two niches, located in the new wall on each side of the stone steps, provide spaces for displaying plants and holiday decorations. The Starksboro Friendship Homemaker's Club bought plants for Memorial Day, as they plan to do annually, and cared for them throughout the summer. The Three-Leaf Clover 4-H Club provided Halloween and Christmas decorations.

American Legion Post No. 19 presented the town with a granite memorial and a 35-foot steel flagpole in honor of the Veterans

*Town Offices, 1973 (A4) and U.S. Post Office, 1976 (A5)*

of All Wars. A large, all-weather flag was provided by the Post and will be replaced when necessary. In the spring of 1986 both monument and flagpole were set near the north end of the new stone wall. The Bristol American Legion conducted an inspiring dedication service there on Memorial Day.

At the annual town meeting, March 4, 1986, a sum not to exceed $11,700.00 of Revenue Sharing funds was designated by the voters for an addition to the municipal building. The new addition, completed in the fall of 1986, provides a much needed office with outside entrance for the Board of Listers. The room was furnished with fur-niture purchased with Revenue Sharing money. A spacious storage room for files, supplies, etc., benefits the town clerk, auditors, listers, and other town officials who use the municipal building.

The Bristol Lions Club gave a glass enclosed bulletin board to the town in 1985. The selectmen purchased material for setting it and building a roof over it. Leroy Smith and Harold Bedard donated their labor to complete it and set it at the front of the Municipal Building-Post Office Parking Lot.

In earlier years notable additions were made to the municipal grounds. Most important was the town owned post office which was constructed on town property a

*Town Office Building.*

short distance south of the municipal building in 1976. On March 1, 1977 the voters authorized the moving of the town war memorial from the Starksboro Village Meeting House lawn to the lawn at the municipal building. Local residents donated plants and time to landscape the area around the memorial.

The municipal building, greatly enhanced by the new stone wall, and the post office together with their well kept lawns and the ample blacktopped parking lot shared by the two buildings provide an attractive town center for Starksboro. Its beauty and usefulness is further enhanced by the two war memorials, the flagpole and flag, the stone bench and outdoor bulletin board. Starksboro is, indeed, proud of it!

Bertha B. Hanson
1985 Town Report

# 1986

### The Hoag Mill - Knight House Complex

Nothing in the surrounding country-side prepares one for his first glimpse of the Old Mill Work-shop...Here everything seems placed by a talented hand, so that building and green spaces, smooth texture and coarse, nature and artifact form pleasing patterns," wrote David Bredemeier in an article which appeared in 1969 in the Autumn issue of *Vermont Life*. He was describing Hoag Grist Mill – Knight Farm House complex which is located in Starksboro along the gorge through which Lewis Creek descends over the Great Falls as it flows westward to Lake Champlain.

The property was owned for many years by the Hoags, a Quaker family from Nine Partners, N.Y. Purchased in 1788 by Joseph Hoag who became the most out-standing Quaker in Vermont history, it was then a part of Monkton. The following year Joseph transferred title to his father, Elijah, who, in turn, sold the property in 1793 to David Hoag and Company – his sons David and Elihu and his son-in-law, Stephen Carpenter. In 1797 this section of Monkton was annexed to Starksboro.

David Hoag and Company developed industry along the falls. A gristmill, carding mill, saw mill and iron forge were in opera-tion early in the nineteenth century. Elihu Hoag operated the farm near the falls him-self. The mill rights, however, were leased to others. It was not until after his death that the property was sold out of the Hoag family.

In 1831 Benjamin Knight came into possession of the farm. Town Records indi-cate that the house was built by him prob-ably between 1838 and 1840. The house, architecturally the most outstanding in town, includes both Federal and Greek Revival elements. Its most impressive feature is the recessed front door, topped by a semi-cir-cular fan light and opened by a hand forged latch. The unique carving on the casings is described thus by Peter Hawley and Nancy Boone, Architectural Historians in the Na-tional Register of Historic Places Nomina-tion Form: "Paneled pilasters flanking the door have unusual "capitals" of thin flat boards with cut-outs in the shape of a radi-ating tear-drop pinwheel. The molding on the outer edge of the arched portion of the surround is scored to resemble tiny dentils and the central keystone is ornamented with shallow symmetrical curves cut out along the upper edge."

*Hoag Grist Mill, c.1799.* (4)

The interior exhibits many Greek Revival details including the trim around the front room fireplace. An unusual feature of the kitchen is a white marble slab set into the floor to accommodate the cookstove.

The farm changed hands several times before 1920 when Vesper Thompson, who already owned and operated the grist mill and the saw mill, purchased it. Since he lived across the creek in the "mill house" the Knight house became a tenement for hired help. In 1946 Mr. and Mrs. Robert Adsit, Sr., bought the house together with the outbuildings and the land around them. At about the same time they purchased the gristmill and the land on both sides of the gorge. This was the beginning of their "twenty year labor of love" which so beautifully restored the property. There they operated The Old Mill Workshop where they restored and sold antiques.

The Adsits made only three notable changes in the exterior of the house. A nearby corn barn was moved up to the west wall and covered with the siding from the demolished saw mill. It provides a breezeway with protected out-door seating and a beautiful view of the creek and the surrounding country. A narrow porch, supported by massive timbers from the saw mill, was added at the lower level of the house facing the creek. The green venetian type shutters, most of which were missing, were replaced with new shutters of plank type construction. Mr. Adsit specially mixed "that just right tint of blue paint" – the color of Chicory blossoms – that now covers them.

Down river from the house on the same side of the stream are two outbuildings. The former hay barn is used for storage. The "hog pen", a barn set on a stone foundation at the creek's edge, has been converted into an apartment.

The gristmill, standing downstream and across the creek from the other buildings, is set into the south side of the gorge. David Bredemeier writes, "The predominant note is set by the huge creek stones of which the mill is built...The creek side view truly awes. Here stone walls rise three stories above the creek bed, massive, handsome and true." Laid in random ashlar, these walls are, indeed, impressive.

The first mention of the gristmill appears in 1799 when Stephen Carpenter, selling a share of the property to his partners excluded his right in "the stone mill on the falls" and his mill privilege on Lewis Creek.

The mill remained in the Hoag family until 1831. After that it changed hands frequently. In 1895 or 1896 a fire destroyed the late 18th century mill works and attic story.

*Old Bridge near Millhouse Bed & Breakfast.*

*Home of Benjamin Knight,*
*c.1838.* (4)

*Millhouse Bed and Breakfast.* Now owned by Ron & Pat Messer. **(4)**

During reconstruction the floors at the second floor and attic level were raised about three feet. A new center door was cut through the stone wall on the south side. This replaced the original door at the west end of the same wall. The old doorway was filled in with fieldstones. At the attic level, just above the new front door, a board and batten door flanked by two windows was installed. Above these the wall was decorated with wooden shingles in a fish scale pattern.

The interior of the mill has been altered several times since the rebuilding in 1896. Vesper Thompson, who purchased the mill in 1904, installed a new turbine and milling rollers about 1912. Robert Adsit removed all milling machinery in 1946 when he con-

verted the building to a wood-working shop. Dr. Ronald Messer, the present owner, has remodeled it for living quarters.

In 1926 Vesper Thompson sold the mill to John Flynn, retaining the right to operate it which he did until his death in 1936. Ten years later Robert Adsit purchased the land and mill. Dr. Ronald Messer bought the Hoag Mill-Knight Farm House complex from the Adsit family in 1971. He now operates the Millhouse Bed and Breakfast there. He has added several stone walls, some of which enclose the site of the old saw mill. These were built for him by David Mason, Starksboro's well-known "artist with stone".

The visual qualities of the Hoag Mill and Knight House complex are outstanding. The Great Falls of Lewis Creek are, themselves, listed as an important fragile area in Addison County. The house is an excellent example of early 19th century residential architecture.

The National Register of Historic Places Nomination Form contains the following statement about the significance of the Hoag Mill. "The grist mill stands as an impressive reminder of the technological accomplishments of early settlers in Vermont. Because it is associated with the Hoag family, the grist mill bears significance not only for the town of Starksboro, but also for the nation, as an example of the ingenuity and industry of Quaker entrepreneurs in 18th century America."

The Hoag Grist Mill – Knight House Complex was listed in The National Register of Historic Places in 1980.

Bertha B. Hanson
1986 Town Report

*Home of Benjamin Knight, c.1838.* **(4)**

117

*Millhouse before and after restoration by the Adsits.* **(4)**

*Dedication &
Biography
Rena W. Tobin
1907-1988*

It is with sadness and pride that we dedicate this issue of our Town Report to Rena White Tobin.

Rena came to Starksboro in 1930. She was the daughter of the then Pastor of the First Baptist Church in Starksboro, the Reverend William White and Anna Fuller White. She and her husband had four children. Phyllis died when she was eight years old. Other children are Norma Wedge of Starksboro, Janet Chamberlain of Proctor and the Reverend Gareth Tobin of Orange and seven grandchildren and five great-grandchildren. Rena had four brothers, the late Norman White, the late Rupert White who grew up in Starksboro, and who was killed in action in World War II, and Howard White of Paterson, New York who married the late Lucy Dike of Starksboro.

In 1931, shortly after moving to Starksboro, Rena joined the First Baptist Church. She immediately became active in church affairs. When a Vacation Bible School was organized she directed the music. The choir was of special interest to her. She served as director for many years. At the time the church constitution was revised, she was Chairman of the Revision Committee. When the church was without a pastor in the early 1960's, Rena, as Chairman of the Pulpit Committee, was responsible for securing substitute speakers. In 1964 the Starksboro and Huntington Baptist Churches decided to hire one pastor to serve both congregations. Rena worked diligently to facilitate the project which resulted in the hiring of the present pastor. She continued as Chairman of the Starksboro Pulpit Committee until her death. In 1965 she became Church Treasurer, an office she held for the remainder of her life. She was also a member of the Finance Committee. In later years she organized and taught an adult Sunday School Class. Elected to the office of Deaconess in 1984 she faithfully fulfilled the responsibilities of that office as long as she lived.

Her delightful poetry added a special dimension to Church Christmas parties,

**Home of Ben and Rena Tobin.** *Now home of Janet Gendreau and son.*

dedication services, anniversaries and memorials and to special community activities as well. In 1976 she wrote a humorous play "The Soft Soap Murder." Based on an account of an actual happening in early Starksboro history it was presented as a part of the Town Bicentennial Celebration.

She was a Charter member of the Starksboro Grange in 1941, and remained a Grange member for life.

Rena served the Town of Starksboro as Town Clerk and Treasurer from 1938 to 1941, and as Town Auditor from 1979 to the time of her death. She was employed as bookkeeper at Mountain View Creamery in Starksboro and Hinesburg and later for East-

ern Milk Producers in Hinesburg from 1940 to 1988.

As a person Rena dedicated her life to her children, grandchildren, great-grandchildren, God and Church. In the community she was a friend to all. She always had time to lend an ear to someone's problems, or write a note or poem to uplift a troubled day. Having gone through the loss of a child herself, she could sympathize with a mother's loss. On December 12, 1988, those who knew her, lost a True Friend.

Bertha B. Hanson
Paulita A. Estey
1987 Town Report

*Early Starksboro*
*Starksboro Village Meeting House*
1840-1990

This year the Starksboro Village Meeting House, one of Starksboro's outstanding landmarks, is celebrating the 150th Anniversary of its construction. On May 18, 1838, the Starksboro Village Meeting House Society was deeded two adjacent parcels of land in the center of the village, upon which they had already begun building a meeting house. The society was a union of the three religious denominations in town: the Methodist Episcopals, organized in 1798, the Free Will Baptists, organized in 1821, and the Christian Church. Just a few months earlier at Town Meeting voters had decided to "raise a tax of Four Hundred Dollars for the purpose of furnishing a town room in the basement story of the meeting house contemplated to be built in the village." Town meeting was first held there April 4, 1839. Construction on the building was completed in 1840.

The Meeting House was built in the architectural style preferred by Episcopal and Methodist Episcopal congregations - the Gothic Revival style. The Gothic Revival style, with its pointed arch windows and belfry with pointed cresting, was seen by church leaders as a reminder of humble English country churches and medieval chapels. It is not known who designed the Village Meeting House but it is similar to other churches in Vermont of the same time period, especially those designed by architect John Cain of Rutland.

The interior is distinguished for the high quality craftsmanship of its furnishings and the grain painting that appears on the doors and woodwork. The numbered pews with their paneled doors, once bought and sold like real estate, were built by George Ferguson who had a casket and carriage making shop across the street. Mark G. Hanson built the free standing benches once used in the town room. Two of them are now at the rear of the sanctuary. In 1884, a large, kerosene lamp chandelier, the gift of Cynthia Holcomb, was installed in the sanctuary. Still in use, this impressive chandelier is made up of a circle of fourteen clear glass kerosene lamps suspended under a fourteen-sided mirrored reflector. A bucket of stones in the attic acts as a fulcrum for raising and lowering the lamps. It is said that Sidney Bushnell and Oscar Baldwin went to

Troy, N.Y. to purchase the fine toned bell. For many years the bell was tolled at nine o'clock on the morning following a death in the community. The number of times it was struck made known the age and sex of the deceased.

Until the 1860's the Methodist Episcopals

*The Starksboro Village Meeting House. Located in the center of Starksboro, the Meeting House faces directly on Route 116. Pictured is south side of building.* **(A29)**

Methodists the sole occupants of the Meeting House sanctuary. In 1911, when the town completed a new Town Hall, the basement room became available for church use. A staircase was built for access from the main floor to the old town room. The room was divided into a parlor, dining room and kitchen. In 1916 the original clear glass panes in the sanctuary windows were replaced with opalescent glass and the shutters which had been installed in 1868 were removed. The stained glass windows were given as memorials to prominent members of the congregation. One is dedicated to Rev. Elijah Hedding, D.D., the seventh Bishop of the Methodist Episcopal Church in America. Hedding came to Starksboro in 1791 with his parents at age 11. Through the encouragement of Mrs. Abraham Bushnell, a Methodist who asked him to read sermons for services in her home, he committed his life to Christ. Baptized beside

used the church half the time, the Free Will Baptists one-fourth of the time, and the Christian Church one-fourth of the time. In 1869 the Baptists built their own church, a large two-story Greek Revival style structure, across the street. The Christian Church eventually lost its membership, thus leaving the

the brook east of Starksboro village, he became an itinerant preacher at age 19. In 1824 he was elected Bishop and served the Troy Conference until his death in 1852.

Over the years membership in the Methodist Episcopal Church fell steadily from a high of 228 in 1842 to a low of 8 in

1914. In 1919 the Society in Starksboro became inactive. The Village Meeting House gradually fell into disrepair. In 1957 Ruth Hanson and her husband, Amos, were instrumental in organizing a community group which revitalized the Meeting House Society. Much needed maintenance and restoration work was begun immediately. The roof was repaired, the sanctuary papered and the downstairs rooms painted. During the next few years the sanctuary was re-carpeted, a new furnace was installed and a bathroom was added. When it became evident that extensive structural repair was needed, generous financial aid from the townspeople funded the project. In 1957 the top section of the steeple, damaged beyond repair, was removed. A bicentennial grant received in 1976 made it possible to rebuild it, thus restoring the steeple to its original appearance. Stone walls enclosing the gardens on each side of the front entrance were designed and built by David Mason. In 1985 the Meeting House was placed on the National Register of Historic Places in recognition of its architectural significance. The Society received a matching grant of $3,100 in 1987 from the Vermont Division for Historic Preservation to replace the leaking roof on the north side of the church with a standing seam metal room and to repair the belfry.

Although regular services are no longer held in the Meeting House, there are special services for Independence Day, Thanksgiving, a Christmas candlelight service and two Sunday services during the summer. The Society also hosts concerts, historical events, an annual sugar-on-snow party the first Sunday in March, and a ham dinner on the first Saturday of October. The building is also used by other groups. The Starksboro Cooperative Preschool held classes there for several years and the Town Library was first housed there. This winter meals for the elderly have been served in the dining room each Monday noon.

The south front window which was not dedicated to anyone has been inscribed with the names of Ruth and Amos Hanson. It is a fitting memorial to their devotion to the work of preserving this architecturally and historically significant building so aptly described by Elizabeth Kirkness in the Burlington Free Press July 2, 1971 as Starksboro's "old meeting house whose roots are deep in the past and which faces toward a bright future."

Bertha B. Hanson and
Elsa Gilbertson
1988 Town Report

*Thelma Bedard*
*Town Clerk &*
*Treasurer*

Thelma Bedard was born in Stowe, Vermont on November 11, 1927, the daughter of Clarence and Jessie Silver. She received her education in Stowe.

In 1944 Thelma came to Starksboro to live with her aunt, Sara Prescott. On March 1, 1946 she married Winston G. Wedge, also of Starksboro. They had four children. Judy and her husband, Bruce Perlee, live in Bristol. Erle, a Chief Petty Officer in the U.S. Navy, and his wife Julie, live in Newport, Rhode Island. Portia Wedge Ploof lives in St. Johnsbury. George Wedge died November 29, 1969, one day before his 17th birthday. There are five grandchildren.

Thelma married for the second time on August 19, 1975 to Harold Bedard of Bristol. She also has five step sons.

She has been a member of the Starksboro Volunteer Fire Department Auxiliary for many years.

From 1980 to 1984 Thelma was Secretary-Treasurer of the Green Mountain Cemetery Association, Inc.

Thelma served as assistant to Ruby Craig from 1959 to 1964. She became Town Clerk and Treasurer in 1964 and has remained in that capacity to the present, except for one year that she lived and was employed in Burlington.

Thelma's years of service were characterized by change. When she was elected to office in 1964 she conducted the town's business in her home. The safes in which the Town Records were stored were housed in a former garage, then located west of the present Municipal building. During the next few years the volume of work which had to be done by the Town Clerk and Treasurer increased rapidly. By 1973, when the present Municipal Building was completed, the job had become full time with regular office hours. Increasing town business made it necessary to add another room to the Municipal Building in 1986.

The most traumatic experience of her years in office occurred Saturday, March 17, 1984. Early in the morning it was discovered that the Municipal Building, along with Robinson School and the Town Hall, had been forcibly entered during the preceding night. The vault in the Town Clerk's Office was broken open and a large sum of money, partially covered by insurance, was stolen. Those responsible were never apprehended.

Due to illness, Thelma will not be a candidate for office this March. Her ready smile made all feel welcome in the Town Clerk's Office. We will truly miss her.

Well done, Good and Faithful Servant.

Bertha Hanson & Paulita Estey
1989 Town Report

Citizenship Award
This certifies that
*Olive Brown Hanson*
has been awarded this Certificate
for being Starksboro's
Most Senior Citizen
July 27, 1991

Today we are proud to honor Olive Hanson who is the oldest resident of Starksboro. Olive Jane Brown, daughter of Perley and Viola (Thompson) Brown, was born May 26, 1904, in the house on States Prison Hollow Road which now belongs to the Katie Thompson family. Her father then operated the old Hoag Grist Mill.

Olive's family roots go deeply into the history of our town. She is descended from two of the four Hill brothers who came from Barrington, New Hampshire to settle in Hillsborough about 1800. Lemuel Hill, her great-great grandfather, built the house where the Olsons now live. His son, Deacon John True Hill, chairman of the building committee for the Free Will Baptist Church, gave unstintingly of time and money to complete that building – a project which was very dear to his heart.

Lemuel's brother, Samuel, Olive's great-great-great grandfather, owned and operated a sawmill near the twin bridges.

Another ancestor, her great-great grandfather, David Brown, who lived on the first farm north of Starksboro Village, was a second generation descendant of the Brown family who settled on Brown Hill.

Deacon David Mason, her great-great grandfather, came to Starksboro from Northfield, New Hampshire about 1812, settling on Mason Hill. Among several family members who accompanied him was his son-in-law, Jethro Stokes, who was Olive's great-great grandfather. He taught the first school on Mason Hill.

Another great-great grandfather, Samuel Thompson, operated an up and down sawmill on the stream which flows down Stokes Hill.

In 1816, the year known as "eighteen hundred and froze to death", Moses Smith, also a great-great grandfather of Olive's, came from New Hampshire. He settled on Shaker Hill on the place now owned by the Craig family.

Olive Brown and Hervey Hanson, great-great grandson of George Bidwell, first settler of the town as chartered, were married September 18, 1920 at the Baptist Parsonage in Starksboro. Most of their married life was spent in this town. It is here that their eight children, three sons – Clifford, Edwin, and Winifred, and five daughters – Ada Pierce, Laura Burritt, Betty Norris, Lois Burbank, and Flora Norris, grew up.

Olive has always been active in the community. She belongs to both the Friendship Homemakers Club and the Christian Culture Club. A member of the Baptist Church, she has, as financial secretary, for many years prepared a careful accounting of the weekly church income.

Everyone – family, neighbors, and friends – is welcome to her home at all times. Wherever and whenever help is needed she is available, giving unstintingly of her time and expertise. Well known for her delicious cooking, she has built a very successful home business for herself. Whenever food is needed for food sales, suppers, or other events she contributes a more than generous amount.

It is a great pleasure for me, as Chairman of the Starksboro Bicentennial Committee, to give this well-deserved certificate of good citizenship to Olive Hanson, a lady who is loved and respected by everyone – and who is to me personally a wonderful mother-in-law.

*Olive Hanson*

Bertha B. Hanson
1990 Town Report

127

## Paulita A. Estey

Paulita Estey was born May 14, 1920 in Middlebury, the daughter of Dr. Peter and Rose (Leddy) Dorey. Her mother died soon after her birth. Her Uncle and Aunt, Thomas and Margaret Conway of Starksboro, moved to the Dorey home to help care for Paulita, her brother and sister.

When Paulita was seven the Conway's returned to Starksboro, bringing Paulita with them. They lived on a farm south of Starksboro Village in the oldest house in town – now Muriel Brown's apartment house. Paulita started her school career in Middlebury Graded School. The move to the one room rural school in Starksboro Village was a traumatic experience. She often said that one of the things she missed the most during her early years in Starksboro was electric lights – everything was so dark!

After completing the eighth grade she enrolled in Bristol High School. She lived at home, going to Bristol on the early morning stage and returning on the stage late in the afternoon. She graduated with honors in 1937 at the age of seventeen.

On her twenty-first birthday, May 14, 1941, she became Postmaster in Starksboro. Her office (since demolished) was in a small building located just south of the old store which is now the resident of Robert St. Amour.

Paulita Dorey and Fenwick Estey were married April 12,1948. In 1949 they bought the Village house which was their home until 1984 when they moved to the trailer on the hill. Fenwick remodeled the north room for use as post office. By fall Paulita was well established in the room that was to be the Starksboro Post Office until 1963 when Fenwick again remodeled the house to accommodate the office on the south end of the building.

Paulita successfully managed both her home and her office during the years when the five Estey children were growing up. The office prospered. Postal services were always available regardless of the hour. The Esteys believed in serving the public.

She served as Postmaster for thirty-two years, retiring December 31, 1972. Always active in postal organizations, she was president and a fifty year member of the National Association of Postmasters. For twenty years she served as secretary-treasurer of the Vermont Chapter of NAPUS Retired.

Busy as she was with her home and office, she always found time for community service. She was active in the PTA, Chairman of Civil Defense,secretary of the Starksboro Aqueduct Company, and Chairman of the Starksboro Democratic Party. She was also a past chairman of the March of Dimes and the Red Cross. One of the founders of the Fire Department Auxiliary, she worked tirelessly on their projects. Many people knew her best as dispatcher for the Fire Department. Her services as a member of the Town Bicentennial Committees for the National Celebration in 1976, the State Constitutional Bicentennial in 1977, and the Statehood Bicentennial in 1991 were indispensable. The most important of all her community services, however, was the help and sympathetic understanding she gave her friends and neighbors in times of need.

After retiring as Postmaster she held several town offices. In 1977 she became an auditor, a position which she occupied for the remainder of her life. She became a Justice of the Peace in 1981. In 1986 she was appointed to the Town Planning Commission. When Interim Subdivision Regulations were adopted she became the Administrative Officer. A member of St. Jude Roman Catholic Church in Hinesburg, she was past president of the Parish Council. For many years she taught Catechism. As a member of the Ladies of St. Jude she worked unceasingly to raise money for a project which was dear to her heart – the building of the beautiful edifice which now serves the parish.

Paulita loved her family, her church, and her town. She served them faithfully and well throughout her life.

Bertha Hanson
1991 Town Report

*Bertha Hanson and Paulita Estey at Town Meeting.*

Joseph Hoag, a Quaker from Nine Partner's, New York, purchased land in the "new country", as Vermont was then called, in the late 1780s. He settled near the present Green Mount Cemetery in what was then the Town of Monkton. Finding land more to his liking in Charlotte, he sold his Monkton holdings, which included the Great Falls of Lewis Creek, to his brothers, David and Elihu, and his brother-in-law, Stephen Carpenter. They proceeded to develop the water power at the falls and expand their holdings. By 1797 they had acquired two first division lots in Starksboro adjacent to the old Monkton-Starksboro town line. David and Elihu deeded their shares of this property to Stephen Carpenter April 18, 1799. It was there, east of the present intersection of states Prison Hollow Road and Route No. 116, that Stephen and Hannah (Hoag) Carpenter built their home.

First they built a small house with low ceilings. A narrow stairway led to sleeping quarters above. The cellar boasted the same type of beautiful stone work which is to be seen in the Hoag Grist Mill foundation. A unique feature was the incorporation of a large boulder, probably already on the site, in the east wall. The cellar had one disadvantage, however. In spring time, then as now, water cascaded over the "big stone" and, despite a drain, made it necessary to build storage bins well above the cellar bottom. Olive Hanson, who spent many of her childhood years there, remembers that her father wore boots when he went to get the potatoes which were always stored there.

Settlement in that section of town progressed rapidly. In 1797 a mile wide strip, including the Great Falls of Lewis Creek, was set off from Monkton to Starksboro. The Hoag and Carpenter families formed the nucleus of a Quaker settlement extending from the States Prison Hollow turn northward to the foot of Wyman Hill, westward to the new Monkton Line and eastward to the foot of Varney Hill. A Quaker Meeting House was built in the present Green Mount Cemetery in 1812. The Starksborough Monthly Meeting of Friends, which eventually included Lincoln, Creek (South Starksboro), and Montpelier as well as the local meeting, was soon established. The meeting continued until 1850 when it was "laid down". In the winter of 1858-59 the Meeting House was sold and moved by ox team to Charlotte, where it was rebuilt as Our Lady of Mount Carmel Roman Catholic Church.

Industries at the Great Falls prospered. Louis Tabler, a grandson of the Carpenter's,

***Home of Stephen Carpenter, c.1810.*** *Brother-in-law to David and Elihu Hoag who owned the Grist Mill.* **(13)**

who became a prominent Ohio Quaker, wrote a poem entitled *Lewis Creek* in which he described the stream at the falls.

> *Working away with a resolute will*
> *Wheeling the factory, turning the mill,*
> *Lifting the hammer or driving the saw,*
> *Turning the lathe and impelling the plane.*

As the Carpenter family prospered and grew it became imperative that they have more living space. They built a so-called I-house which they attached to the west end of their first home. The new house was long and narrow. From the center doorway, located on the long side of the house facing west, a steep, narrow stairway with a simple side rail led to the second floor. On the south side of the lower hall was the parlor with a fireplace framed with a plain, very attractive mantle, which is still in place. The room above also had a fireplace. In later years that room was occupied by Olive Hanson's great-aunt, Olive Hill. "Aunt Olive" as she was known to all her young relatives, kept a music box on the mantle. Anna (Ferguson) White, wife of the Rev. W. W. White, former minister of the Starksboro Baptist Church, delighted in hearing it play when she was a child.

Louis Taber, born in 1811, told his daughter how, as a child, he whiled the hours away watching the "finny tribe" in the placid Mill Pond lying near his grandfather's doorstep. In his poem, *Lewis Creek*, he vividly described the simple pleasures of childhood in the valley:

*In childhood oft, I stole away,*
*With schoolmates, on Thy banks to stray,*
*Gathering lilies on Thy bank,*
*Stooping down Thy waters to drink*
*Climbing the willows by Thy side,*
*Bathing in Thy silver tide;*
*Upon Thy bosom, proud to float,*
*On fragile craft, or in tiny boat.*
*With bounding boys, let loose from school,*
*How the skates flew o'er Thy crystal pool!*
*Or, mirthfully gliding o'er and o'er,*
*Back and forth on thy glassy floor.*
*And strange, weird shapes of beauty stood,*
*The genii of Thy frost bound flood.*

Stephen Carpenter and his wife, Hannah, died in the early 1830s. Their sons, David and Elihu, inherited the property. Elihu deeded his share to David. In 1835, after David's death, Amos Battey, Administrator, sold the place to James Chase, a Quaker from Bristol. James and his wife, Ruth, continued to live there until 1858 when they moved to Iowa to join several of their children who had already settled there.

(Deacon) John True Hill purchased the property on May 29, 1858. Together with his wife, Alvina (Hill), he operated one of the most successful farms in the area. Alvina was an expert weaver and an outstanding cheese maker. Her cheese was made in the back room of the old house and cured in the north room above the carriage shed, which had been finished with plastered walls especially for this purpose.

The Hill's were prominent Free Will Baptists. Deacon True, as he was called, was chairman of the building committee for the Free Will Baptist House Association which built the present Baptist Church in Starksboro Village. He gave unstintingly of time and money to the project.

From (Deacon) John True and Alvina the farm descended to their youngest daughter, Susan, and her husband, Ira Brown. Their son, Perley, and his wife, Viola, acquired it in 1921. That year they sold it to Harrison Thompson. The Thompson family occupied it until 1937. John and Mable Dike then owned it until 1942, when Frederick and Evelyn Jennings and Clinton and Esther Jennings, two brothers and their wives, bought it. It later became the sole property of Clinton and Esther who sold it to Arthur and Vera Cota. It is now owned by the R. J. Colton Company.

The house, listed in the State Register of Historic Places, is part of the Hoag Mill Complex. One of the town's most historic homes, it is an outstanding example of Federal architecture. The rare carriage shed adds an air of distinction to the place. Surprisingly unchanged through the years, the interior appointments provide an authentic picture of the home of a successful Vermont farmer in the last century.

Bertha B. Hanson
1992 Town Report

132

*Bertha Brown Hanson*

T he Town of Starksboro lost one of it most faithful and dedicated public officials on December 1, 1994, with the passing of Bertha Brown Hanson. Bertha was born on August 30, 1917, to Anson and Sylvia (Hill) Brown and spent her childhood in Huntington and Starksboro. Many town residents grew up with Bertha and attended school with her in the North School on State's Prison Hollow Road. She spent her senior year at the Friends School in Poughkeepsie, New York. She then went on to earn her bachelor of arts from Earlham College in Richmond, Indiana and master's degree in American History from Claremont College in Claremont, California. Upon returning home, she taught at several Vermont schools, including Black River Academy in Ludlow and the Quechee School.

On November 14, 1947, she married Clifford W. Hanson. Throughout their life together they operated a dairy farm in Starksboro, Monkton and Huntington. Clifford passed away on April 12, 1994. Four children survive her; Mark and his wife Susan, Stephen, Sylvia and Olive Phillips and her husband Jeffrey; and four grandchildren, Jolene and Mathias Hanson and Julie and Daniel Phillips. A son, Andrew, and a grandson, Adam Hanson, predeceased her.

Bertha began her public service in 1948, when she was elected to the position of auditor, a post she held the rest of her life. She and others who served with her, including Ruby Craig, were noted for their accuracy and eye for detail. For many years they were rewarded for their efforts by winning the James P. Taylor Memorial Town Report Contest Award of Excellence, sponsored by the Vermont State Agency of Administration and the UVM Extension Service.

Bertha began writing entries on Starksboro history for the Town Report in 1954. These fascinating articles, with accompanying historic photographs, focused on such topics as Starksboro schools, early industry and historic buildings.

In the mid-1960s Bertha was on the committee that studied whether Starksboro should join the effort to build Mount Abraham Union High School in Bristol. The school opened in 1967 and she served on the board of directors until her death, traveling to Bristol three and four times a month for 27 years.

Bertha also was a member of the Starksboro Planning Commission since 1972 and for many years was on the Addison County Regional Planning Commission. Her service was faithful until the end; the evening before her passing she was attending a Regional Planning Commission meeting.

As a Justice of the Peace, Bertha served on the Board of Civil Authority. She was always found at the polling place on Election Day and Town Meeting Day and occasionally she was called on to perform marriage ceremonies.

The church was an important part of Bertha's life. She was a faithful member of the First Baptist Church and also attended services at the South Starksboro Friends Meeting House. At the Baptist Church she always could be found sitting in her family's pew, which they bought when the church was built in 1869. For 25 years she assisted Reverend Martens by preparing the bulletin for Sunday. She also prepared the communion and was an active participant in Bible study groups.

Bertha was probably best known for her love of history. She was the chairman of town committees that planned the celebration for the United States Bicentennial in 1976 and Vermont's Bicentennial in 1991. She was the

one everyone turned to for information on local genealogy, but she was also a scholar with a profound knowledge of the broader history of Starksboro, surrounding towns, and Vermont as a whole. Best of all she knew how to make history fun and delighted in sharing her knowledge with others. Bertha made history interesting and relevant, describing events that happened 50, 100, or 200 years ago so they came alive. She gave a number of programs on local history at the Village Meeting House, Starksboro Public Library, and in surrounding communities.

Bertha knew that local history is important and that it provides us with a sense of place and belonging. When she drove around, she could see history everywhere. As she traveled to and from her home farm she saw the farmers driving their wagons full of corn and wheat to the old grist mill on the Great Falls of the Lewis Creek. She saw the village iron foundry at work, the Irish immigrants settling on Ireland Road and the butter tubs and cheese boxes being made

*Bertha counting ballots - Election Day, Nov. 1994.*

in Baldwin's factory on Baldwin Pond above the village.

Historic buildings contributed to the sense of place Bertha loved and wanted to preserve. She was instrumental in working to save and restore area landmark buildings. These include her beloved Union Church in Huntington, the Starksboro Village Meeting House, and the Rokeby Museum in Ferrisburgh where she was on the board for many years. Just the day before she passed away she was planning the annual Meeting House Christmas Candlelight service and discussing the next restoration project for the building.

Bertha's love of family, church, friends, community, and history was evident in her dedicated community service. She knew from whence we had come and strove to ensure continued community vitality and well-being, not only for the children and grandchildren she was so proud of and delighted in but for everyone. She was a great treasure. We knew her, we loved her, and we will forever miss her.

Elsa Gilbertson
1993 Town Report

*View of Clifford and Bertha Hanson's Farm Buildings - 1940s. House c.1873.* **(1)**

*View of Mark and Susan Hanson's home from the mountainside -1940s. House c.1800/c.1835.* **(2)**

*Home of Clifford and Bertha Hanson, c.1910. Pictured are Bertha's parents: Anson and Sylvia Brown with horses.* **(1)**

*Mark and Susan Hanson's House - Calvin & Mary Clifford in front. c. 1900.* **(2)**

*Village scene looking North - Starksboro Village.* **(A34** *on left,* **A8** *on right)*

*Taking Maple Syrup to the Railroad in Bristol.*

*Starksboro Band.*

*Route 116 South of the Village where road was blasted through ledges.*

***Rodman Richard Hill House.*** *Rodman R. Hill and his wife Sarah. Now home of Ralph &
Cathy Mashburn.*

***Rte 116 South. Now home of Delwin & Margot Gilley. House c.1840.*** **(43)**

*Gwendolyn Merrill's House, c.1860.* Most houses at the north end of Starksboro were not built until after the middle of the nineteenth century. Now home of Bryan & Gina Merrill. **(A42)**

*Heading North out of Starksboro Village c. 1900.*

*Greta Knox House, c.1865/
1840. Owned by Mitchell
Horner/Robin Hendee.* **(A31)**

***Fourth of July
Celebration.*** *Probably in
the early 1900s.*

***Workshop in Village,
c.1900.*** *Blacksmith shop
across from Robinson
School.* **(A21e)**

*Jim Dwire Homestead, Jerusalem.*

**Jim Dwire Homestead,** *Jerusalem.*

*Home of Leroy and Ila Smith. House c.1835/c.1880. Then Wayne Place. Now home of John and Colleen Whitten.* **(A39)**

*Village scene in Starksboro looking north from Meeting House.*

Sites listed in the State
Register of Historic Places
Numbers correspond to Register
listing that follow.
*(For **A** see historic district map.)*

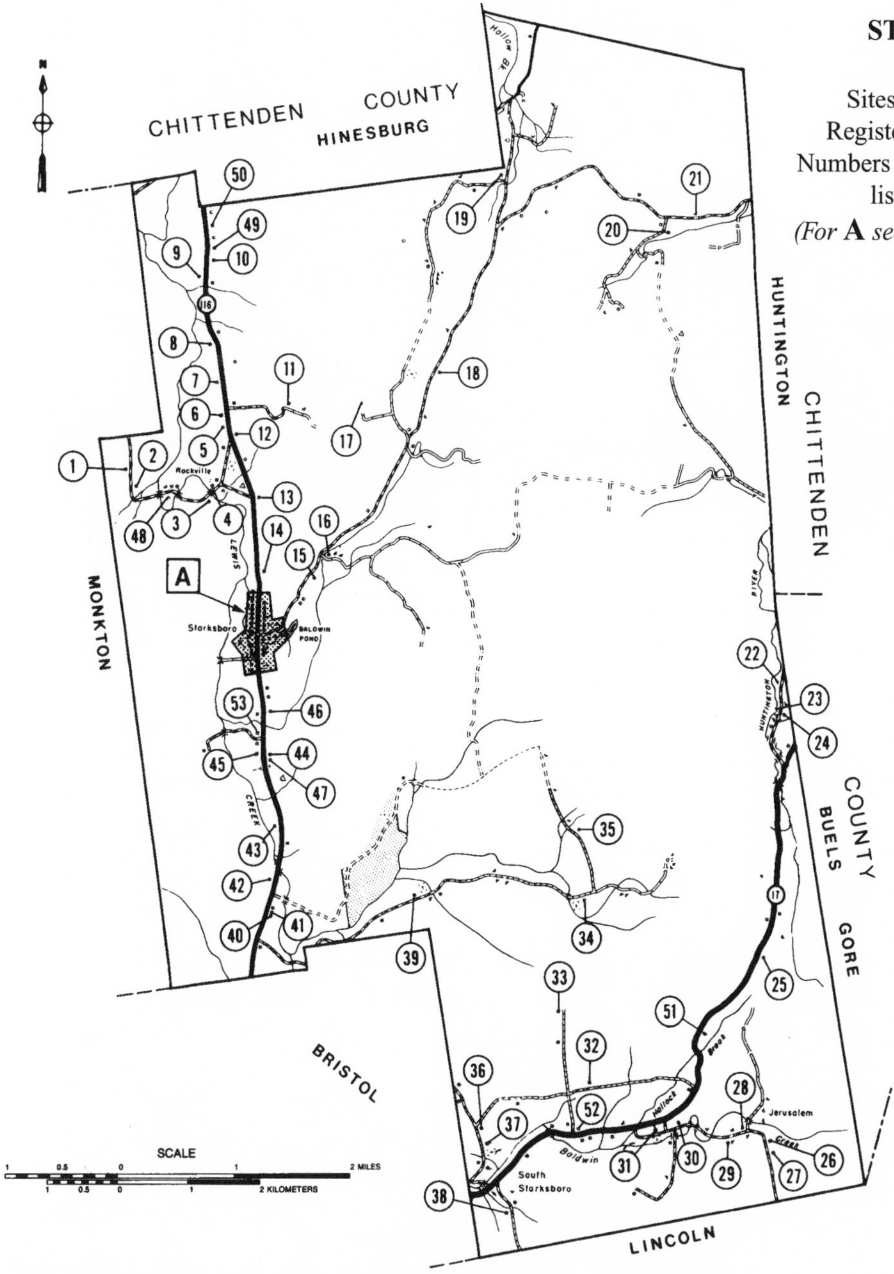

SCALE

SOURCE: VT. AGENCY OF TRANSPORTATION GENERAL HIGHWAY MAP, 1979.

147

**TOWN OF STARKSBORO** Sites listed in the State Register of Historic Places (For locations see town and historic district maps.)

**1-** House, c.1873 Vernacular-Italianate style, gable roof, 1.5 stories. Features: peaked lintel-boards, Italianate porch. Related shed.

**2-** House, c.1800/c.1835 Greek Revival

style, Classic Cottage . Features: enriched entablature, sidelights, corner pilasters, entry pilasters, full entablature. Related shed.

**3-** House, c.1820 Gable roof, 2 stories. Features: sidelights, entry entablature, Italianate porch. Related shed, early bank barn.

**4-** Hoag Gristmill
a. Mill, c.1799 Stone, gable roof, 2 1/2 stories. Features: shinglework.
b. House, c.1838 Vernacular-Federal style, gable roof, 13/4 stories. Features: central chimney, distinctive door, keystone, cornerblocks, entry pilasters, entry fanlight.
c. Stable, c.1850 Features: bank of windows.
d. Pighouse, c.1850 *Listed in the National Register of Historic Places.*

**5-** House, c.1835 Vernacular-Greek Revival style, Classic Cottage. Features: entry entablature, entry pilasters, transom, Queen Anne porch. Related shed, shed.

**6-** Early Barn, c.1850 Gable roof, 1.5 stories. Related shed, shed, shed.

**7-** House, c.1840 Vernacular-Greek Revival style, Classic Cottage. Features: sidelights, entry entablature, kneewall window. Related stable.

**8-** House, c.1880/c.1900 Italianate style, hip roof, 2 stories. Features: porte cochere, Italianate porch, cornice brackets, distinctive lintelboards, Colonial Revival porch. Related barn, farm shop, stable. Features: cupola, ventilators, hoist.

**9-** House, c.1870 Classic Cottage. Features: peaked lintelboards, peaked entry lintel.

**1O-** House, 1809 Cape Cod. Features: cornice brackets, cornice caps, sidelights. Related stable, ground stable barn, shed.

**11-** House, c.1850 Classic Cottage. Features: kneewall window, entry entablature.

**12-** House, c.1810/c.1880 Hip roof, 2

stories. Features: entry pilasters, Queen Anne porch, cornice caps, distinctive door, kneewall window. Related ground stable barn, milkhouse, pumphouse. Features: hoist.

**13-** House, c.1810 Vernacular-Federal style, I-House. Features: entry entablature, transom, continuous architecture. Related carriage barn. Features: carriage bays.

**14-** House, c.1860 Greek Revival style, sidehall plan, 2 stories. Features: distinctive chimney, full entablature, entry pilasters, gable fanlight, sunburst. Related early bank barn.

**15-** House, c.1870 Gable roof, 11/2 stories. Features: Gothic Revival porch, distinctive door, peaked lintelboards. Related stable.

**16-** House, c.1810 Vernacular-Federal style, gable roof, 1.5 stories. Features: cornerblocks, distinctive door, label lintels, fluted corner pilasters, fluted entry pilasters, continuous architecture. Related carriage barn.

**17-** House, c.1850 Gable roof, 1.5 stories. Related early bank barn.

**18-** House, c.1865 Gable roof, 1.7 stories. Features: cornice caps, kneewall window.

**19-** House, c.1820 Georgian plan. Features: Colonial Revival porch. Related ground stable barn, farm shop.

**20-** School, c.1830 Gable roof, 1.5 stories. Features: cornice caps, cast-iron, door hood. Related garage.

**21-** House, c.1870 Gable roof, 1.5 stories. Features: peaked lintelboards.

Related late bank barn.

**22-** House, c.1850 Classic Cottage.

**23-** School, c.1832/1904 Gable roof, 1.5 stories. Features: bank of windows.

**24-** House, c.1870 Gable roof, 1.5 stories. Related stable.

**25-** House, c.1865 Vernacular-Greek Revival style, Classic Cottage. Features: peaked lintelboards, entry entablature. Related carriage barn.

**26-** House, c.1865 Gable roof, 1.5 stories. Features: peaked lintelboards, peaked entry lintel. Related early barn.

**27-** House, c.1850 Vernacular-Greek Revival style, Classic Cottage. Features: entry entablature, bay window, raking window, full entablature. Related early barn, carriage barn, shed.

**28-** House, c.1870 Gable roof, 1.5 stories. Features: Bungalow porch, peaked lintelboards.

**29-** House, c.1860 Greek Revival style, sidehall plan, 1.5 stories. Features: sidelights, entry enta-blature, entry pilasters, peaked lintelboards.

**30-** (Farm)
a. House, c.1860 Gable roof, 2.5 stories. Features: Queen Anne porch, peaked lintelboards.
b. Early Bank Barn, c.1870
c. Chicken Coop, c.1925
d. Garage, c.1930 Hip roof.
e. Stable, c.1905 f. Shed, c.1950

**31-** School, 1874/1904 Gable roof, 1.5 stories. Features: bank of windows, door hood, segmental arch window, cemetery.

**32-** (Farm)
a. House, c.1920 Hip roof, 2 stories. Features: Colonial Revival porch. b. Early Bank Barn, c.1870 Features: continuous architecture, hoist.
c. Barn, c.1880
d. Sugarhouse, c. 1970 Features: ventilator.
e. Ice House, c.1900 Wood shingle. f. Milkhouse, c.1925
g. Chicken Coop, c.1910
h. Chicken Coop, c.1910
i. Garage, c.1930 Hip roof.
j. Early Barn, c.1850 Features: continuous architecture.

**33-** House, c.1860 Vernacular-Greek Revival style, Classic Cottage. Features: entry entablature, full entablature.

**34-** School, 1896 Gable roof, 1.5 stories. Related cemetery.

**35-** House, c.1810 Federal style, Georgian plan. Features: entry entablature, cornice caps. Related shed.

**36-** House, c.1810 Federal style, Georgian plan. Features: entry entablature, entry pilasters, triangular gable fanlight, sidelights, Italianate porch. Related shed, ground stable barn. Features: ventilators, weathervane .

**37-** Meetinghouse, 1826/1871 Gable roof, 1 story. Features: entry entablature, cornice caps. *Listed in the National Register of Historic Places.*

**38-** (Farm)
a. House, c.1810 Federal style, Georgian plan. Features: entry entablature, sidelights, entry pilasters.
b. Early Bank Barn, c.1865
c. Sugarhouse, c. 1980
d. Shop, c.1870
e. Sugarhouse, c. 1910

**39-** House, c.1885 Classic Cottage. Features: kneewall window, Italianate porch. Related farm shop, stable, shed.

**40-** House, c.1860 Vernacular-Greek Revival style, Classic Cottage. Features: Italianate porch, corner pilasters, entry pilasters, sidelights, kneewall window. Related garage.

**41-** House, c. 1835 Federal style,

pavilion with ells. Features: Palladian window, sidelights, distinctive chimney.

**42-** (Farm)
a. House, c.1850 Greek Revival style, Classic cottage. Fatures: sidelights, entry entablature, entry pilasters, corner pilasters, full entablature, peaked lintelboards, Gothic Revival porch.
b. Farm Shop, c.1976
c. Freestall Barn, c.1960 board and batten.
d. Carriage Barn, c.1850
e. Bank Barn, c.1850
f. Silo, c.1960
g. Ground Stable Barn, c.1900
h. Barn, c.1950

**43-** House, c.1840
Gable roof, 21/2 stories. Features: distinctive door, cornice caps. Related stable.

**44-** House, c.1810 Cape Cod. Features: sidelights. Related early bank barn.

**45-** House, c.1845 Vernacular-Greek Revival style, Classic Cottage. Features: entry entablature, sidelights.

**46-** House, c.1865 Vernacular-Creek Revival style, Classic Cottage. Features: kneewall window, entry entablature, entry pilasters, cornice caps, Queen Anne porch. Related early bank barn.

**47-** House, c.1810 Vernacular-Federal style, Cape Cod. Features: transom, wall pilasters.

**48-** House, c.1830/c.1890 Gable roof, 1.5 stories. Features: Queen Anne porch. Related barn.

**49-** House, c.1840 Vernacular-Greek Revival style, Classic Cottage. Features: corner pilasters, entry entablature, entry pilasters, sidelights.

**50-** House, c.1875 Gable roof, 1.5 stories. Features: round window, slate, cornice caps.

**51-** House, c.1860 Gable roof, 1.5 stories. Features: Queen Anne porch. Related ground stable barn.

**52-** School, c.1850 Gable roof, 1.5

stories. Features: peaked lintelboards, distinctive door, historic move.

**53-** House, 1797/c.1926 Gable roof, 1.5 stories.

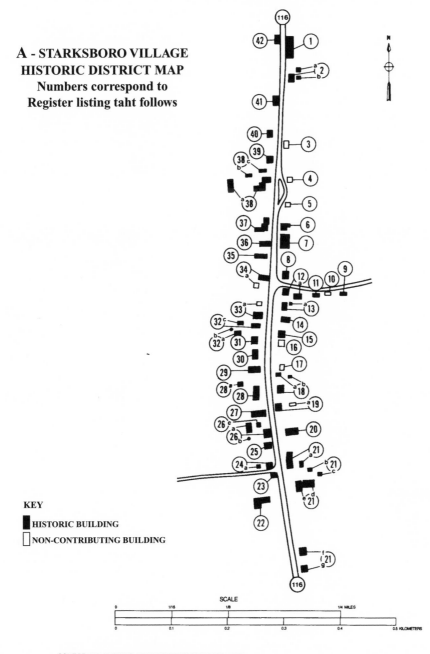

**A - STARKSBORO VILLAGE**
**HISTORIC DISTRICT MAP**
**Numbers correspond to**
**Register listing taht follows**

**KEY**

█ **HISTORIC BUILDING**

☐ **NON-CONTRIBUTING BUILDING**

SCALE

## STARKSBORO VILLAGE HISTORIC DISTRICT

**A1-** Creamery, 1898/c.1940 Gable roof, 1 story.

**A2-** House, c.1865 Gable roof, 11/2 stories. Features: porch.

**A2a-** Garage, c.1930

**A2b-** Shed, c.1930

**A3-** House, c.1978 Non-contributing due to age.

**A4-** Office, 1973 Non-contributing due to age.

**A5** -Post Office, 1976 Non-contributing due to age.

**A6-** House, c.1820 Gable roof, 1 story.

**A7-** Store, c.1850/1865 Greek Revival

style, gable roof, 11/2 stories. Features: peaked lintelboards, Greek Revival storefront, distinctive door.

**A8-** Hotel, c.1835 Greek Revival style, Georgian plan. Features: corner pilasters, peaked lintelboards, sidelights, entry pilasters.

**A9-** House, c.1860 Classic Cottage.

**A10-** Mobile Home, c.1970 Non-contributing due to age.

**A11-** House, c. 1860 Gable roof, 1 story.

**A12-** House, c.1865 Gothic Revival style, gable roof, 2 1/2 stories. Features: bargeboard, cornice caps, distinctive chimney, Gothic wall dormer, Gothic Revival porch.

**A12a** -Early Bank Barn, c.1855

**A13-** House, c.1810/c.1900 Vernacular-Queen Anne style, gable roof, 11/2 stories. Features: shinglework, Queen Anne porch, Queen Anne window.

**A13a-** Garage, c.1925

**A14-** Mill, c.1795/1868 Gable roof, 2 1/2 stories.

**A15-** House, c.1810 Gable roof, 2 stories.

**A16-** House, c.1810 Non-contributing due to alterations.

**A17-** Mobile Home, c.1950 Non-contributing due to age.

**A18-** House, c.1835 Vernacular-Greek Revival style, Georgian plan. Features: sidelights, entry pediment, entry entablature.

**A18a-** Garage, c.1940

**A18b-** Chicken Coop, c.1940

**A19-** House, c.1835 Vernacular-Federal style, I-House. Features: entry entablature.

**A19a-** Shed, c.1960 Non-contributing due to age.

**A20-** Church, 1869 Greek Revival style, gable roof, 2 stories. Features: full entablature, paneled corner pilasters, peaked lintelboards, entry entablature, entry pilasters, ridge tower, belfry.

**A21-** House, c.1840 Greek Revival

style, Georgian plan. Features: paneled corner pilasters, sidelights, paneled entry pilasters, entry entablature, triangular gable fanlight .

**A21a-** Garage, c.1930

**A21b-** Shed, c.1900 Features: transom.

**A21c-** Shop, c.1900

**A21d-** Late Bank Barn, c.1860

**A21e-** Late Bank Barn, c.1900

**A21f-** Carriage Barn, c. 1870

**A21g-** Garage, c.1920

**A22** - School, 1892/1941 Gable roof, 1 1/2 stories. Features: Colonial Revival porch, bank of windows.

**A23-** House, c.1865 Gable roof, 1 1/2 stories. Features: sidelights.

**A24** -House, c.1810 Vernacular-Federal style, Georgian plan. Features: entry entablature, entry pilasters, entry fanlight.

**A24a-** Carriage Barn, c.1890

**A25-** Shop, c.1820 Gable roof, 1 1/2 stories.

**A26-** House, c.1865 Gothic Revival style, Classic Cottage. Features: Gothic wall dormer, queen Anne porch.

**A26a-**Early Bank Barn, c.1850 Features: cornice caps.

**A26b-** Silo, c.1920 Sheet metal.

**A27-** Town Hall, 1911 Gable roof, 2 stories. Features: transom, Queen Anne porch.

**A28-** House, c.1850 Greek Revival style, three-quarter Classic Cottage. Features: entry pilasters, entry entablature, peaked lintelboards, peaked entry lintel, corner pilasters.

**A28a-** Early Bank Barn, c.1840 Features: transom.

**A28b-** Garage,c.1930

**A29-** Meetinghouse, 1840 Gothic

Revival style, gable roof, 1 1/2 stories. Features: distinctive interior, entry entablature, ridge tower, pointed arch window, enriched entablature, stained glass, entry pilasters. *Listed in the National Register of Historic Places*

**A30-** House, c.1800 Cape Cod.

**A31-** House, c. 1865 1840 Classic Cottage. Features: entry pilasters, sidelights.

**A32** -House, c.1880 Vernacular-Queen Anne style, gable roof, 2 1/2 stories. Features: shinglework, Queen Anne porch, bay window.

**A32a-** Garage, c.1932

**A32b-** Silo, c.1950

**A32c-** Early Barn, c.1860

**A33-** House, c.1830/c.1900 Gable roof, 21/2 stories.

**A33a-** Garage, c.1950 Non-contributing due to age.

**A34-** Store, 1860/c.1900 Gable roof, 2 1/2 stories. Features: original storefront, porch.

**A34a-** Garage, c.1950 Non-contributing due to age.

**A35** -House, c.1840/c.1890 Vernacular-Greek Revival style, sidehall plan, 2 stories. Features: sidelights, paneled entry pilasters, Queen Anne porch, triangular gable fanlight .

**A36-** Store, c.1900 Gable roof, 1 1/2 stories.

**A37-** House, c.1840 Greek Revival style, Classic Cottage . Features: full entablature, sidelights, entry entablature, cornice caps, corner pilasters.

**A38-** House, c.1810 Federal style,

I-House. Features: Queen Anne porch, gable fan, distinctive chimney, sidelights, entry fanlight, distinctive door, continuous architecture.

**A38a-** Late Bank Barn, c.1890 Features: ventilators.

**A38b-** Chicken Coop, c.1925

**A38c-** Early Bank Barn, c.1850

**A39** -House, c.1835/c.1880 Vernacular-Queen Anne style, gable roof, 1 1/2 stories. Features: shinglework, door hood.

**A40-** House, c.1840 Gable roof, 1 1/2 stories.

**A41-** Store, 1908 Gable roof, 1 1/2 stories. Features: Commercial storefront.

**A42-** House, c.1860 Classic Cottage. Features: Queen Anne porch, entry entablature, entry pilasters.